HOW
TO
WRITE
A
NOVEL
IN
100 DAYS

WITH TIPS ABOUT AGENTS, EDITORS, PUBLISHERS AND SELF-PUBLISHING

What established writers have said about
How to Write a Novel in 100 Days

ALL ASPIRING WRITERS struggle to balance their writing and working lives, especially in a world filled with digital distractions. In *How to Write a Novel in 100 Days* John Coyne takes us back to the basics with simple time management strategies, actionable writing tips and practical worksheets. A powerful toolkit for time-strapped scribblers.

— Jason Boog
editor of the blog "GallyCat" at MediaBistro.com

■

I HEARD JOHN COYNE give his "How to Write a Novel in 100 Days" lecture several years ago. Despite the good-natured whispers of "snake oil" from the writers in the crowd, we all knew that his formula wasn't a gimmick, but a blueprint for doing what he's done many, many times — and with great success. It is possible to write a novel in 100 days — and John Coyne knows the secret, which he is now sharing.

— Mark Brazaitis
author of *The Incurables: Stories*

■

HOW TO WRITE A NOVEL IN 100 DAYS is the perfect prescription for anyone who has ever dreamed of writing a novel. With quotes from the masters on how they did it and an easy-to-follow road map to a completed manuscript, it's a coach, a guide, and a literary best friend. This is sound, entertaining writing advice, drawn from those who know the journey well. Stick to these steps and you'll have soon climbed the mountain of writing your own book.

— Tony D'Souza
author of *Whiteman* and *Mule*

■

EVERYBODY HAS A GREAT STORY in them, but most of us don't know how to GET THAT STORY OUT. In *How to Write a Novel in 100 Days*, novelist and teacher John Coyne explains — with wit, sass and not just a little bit of inside knowledge — the process that begins with a vague idea and ends happily ever after, i.e., with a published book.

— Sara Nelson
Editorial Director, Amazon.com

∎

I WISH I'D HAD *How to Write a Novel in 100 Days* before I started my latest book. It took me ten years to write this novel.

— Bob Shacochis
author of *The Woman Who Lost Her Soul*

∎

IF JOHN COYNE WILL PLEASE turn his attention to a 100-day diet book, we'll all have arms like Michelle and be sporting bikinis by summer. In *How to Write a Novel in 100 Days* he steers aspiring writers, with clarity and style, up the thrilling spiral staircase that leads to a completed novel, all the while offering crucial cautionary advice against the temptation to take a breather at those kiss-of-death rest stops.

— Mary-Ann Tirone Smith
author of *Girls of Tender Age: A Memoir*

∎

EQUAL PARTS INSTRUCTION, inspiration, and butt-in-the-chair schedule, *How to Write a Novel in 100 Days* will be a gift to anyone who's ever thought she wanted to try to write a novel but didn't know how to go about doing it.

— Rachel Toor
Associate Professor of Creative Writing, Eastern Washington University
and columnist for *The Chronicle of Higher Education*

∎

FOR THOSE LUCKY ENOUGH to know him personally, John Coyne is a renowned cheerleader, travel guide, and birthing coach for the writing endeavors of others, and in *How to Write a Novel in 100 Days* he extends that same jovial kick-in-the-pants to anyone with daring enough to take pen in hand. Through daily writing exercises that seem almost more like treats than tasks, coupled with words of encouragement from literary masters who, like you, once had to figure out how to write their first novel, John will coax that book out of you in no time!

— Ellen Urbani

author of *When I Was Elena*

■

HOW TO WRITE A NOVEL IN 100 DAYS is like a (slightly longer) countdown to New Year's Eve. But at the end of reading John Coyne's inventive and helpful book, you get more than just a hat to wear and champagne to drink. You get a novel you have written with the help of a master. So just start counting down: 100, 99, 98, 97, 96 . . .

— Richard Wiley

author of *Soldiers in Hiding*, winner of the 1986 PEN/Faulkner Award

■

ALSO BY JOHN COYNE

NOVELS

The Caddie Who Won The Masters

The Caddie Who Played with Hickory

The Caddie Who Knew Ben Hogan

Child of Shadows

Fury

The Hunting Season

Brothers & Sisters

The Shroud

Hobgoblin

The Searing

The Piercing

The Legacy

INSTRUCTIONAL

Playing with the Pros

New Golf for Women

Better Golf

This Way Out (with Tom Hebert)

Getting Skilled (with Tom Hebert)

By Hand (with Tom Hebert)

Penland Book of Jewelry Making

Penland Book of Pottery

How to Make Upside-Down Dolls

COLLECTIONS EDITED BY JOHN COYNE

Going Up Country: Travel Essays by Peace Corps Volunteers

Living on the Edge: Fiction by Peace Corps Volunteers

To Touch the World: The Peace Corps Experience

Peace Corps: The Great Adventure

HOW TO WRITE A NOVEL IN 100 DAYS

WITH TIPS ABOUT AGENTS, EDITORS, PUBLISHERS AND SELF-PUBLISHING

JOHN COYNE

A PEACE CORPS WRITERS BOOK

HOW TO WRITE A NOVEL IN 100 DAYS

A PEACE CORPS WRITERS BOOK
An imprint of Peace Corps Worldwide.
Copyright 2013 © by John Coyne
Cover design, book design and layout by Marian Haley Beil

HOW TO WRITE A NOVEL IN 100 DAYS is based on a series by John Coyne
published online at PeaceCorpsWriters.org in 2001

For more information, contact peacecorpsworldwide@gmail.com.
Peace Corps Writers and the Peace Corps Writers colophon
are trademarks of PeaceCorpsWorldwide.org.

Library of Congress Control Number: 2013916041

ISBN-13: 978-1-935925-76-7

FIRST PEACE CORPS WRITERS EDITION, September 2013

This book is dedicated to all first-time novelists.

INTRODUCTION

Do you have a great story that you need to tell? Is there this little nagging voice in the back of your mind that has been saying all your life: "Go ahead and do it. Write your story." After a lifetime of reading other people's books, do you want to start writing one of your own?

If you know you'll never be satisfied until you sit down and write your novel; if you're tired of people saying "You're not a *real* writer"; if you know in your heart that you can do it; then begin. The truth is, all writing begins in the human heart.

But then, how do you unlock what's in your heart and write your novel?

Here's how: You do it in the next 100 days. In that time you will write (and rewrite) your novel by following the simple instructions in this small book. The "how" is the easy part because you will be following a technique I have developed as a writer. It is the technique I have used in the course of writing 12 novels of my own.

Writing is a craft that can be learned. If you follow these 100 days of instruction, you will have a novel that will be publishable by a commercial publisher, academic press or a print-on-demand company that can also make it available as an e-book for the Kindle, the iPad or the Nook. There are many ways to publish a novel, but first you have to write one.

Who is John Coyne and why should I listen to him?

I have published 25 books: fiction, nonfiction, collections, guide books, instructional books. I have written award-winning and best-selling novels of mystery, horror, romance, historical fiction and sports. My novels have been published in many foreign countries.

I also wrote seven novels before publishing my first one, and could paper a wall with the rejection slips I have received from some of the best magazines and publishing companies in the world.

I earned Bachelor and Master of Arts degrees in English literature, and have taught creative writing at the high school and college levels, as well as on the Internet. I have published articles in such national magazines as *Smithsonian*, *Glamour*, *Redbook* and *Travel & Leisure*; my short stories have been included in a half-dozen anthologies. I've written for a wide range of newspapers, including the *Washington Post* and the *Chicago Tribune*. I have conducted writing workshops in a dozen U.S. cities, and taught English and writing in Africa.

My latest book, *The Caddie Who Won The Masters*, was published in 2011. It is the third in a successful series of novels that take place in the world of professional golf. Many of my novels are available as e-books that you can find on Amazon.com. You can learn more about me and my books on my website at www.JohnCoyneBooks.com.

I am well connected in the publishing industry, and know what it takes to be published. The advice I give in this book will help you write *your* novel — a novel that might make it possible for you to quit your job and write full-time. It has happened to other writers I know; it could happen to you.

How many times have you finished reading a book and said to yourself, "I could have written that?" We all carry around within ourselves at least one book. Nobel Prize-winning novelist Toni Morrison has put it this way: "If there's a book you really want to read but it hasn't been written yet, then you must write it."

The only two things you need to write a novel are: the ability to write a simple English sentence and the desire to write. You can do it.

Writing and working

It's hard to find time to write when you have a full-time job, a family and other responsibilities. Most writers have had to carry on two lives. The poet Wallace Stevens was vice president of an insurance company and an expert on the bond market. The young T. S. Eliot was a banker. William Carlos Williams, a pediatrician. Robert Frost, a poultry farmer. Hart Crane packed candy in his father's warehouse and later wrote advertising copy. Stephen Crane was a war correspondent. Marianne Moore worked at the New York Public Library, James Dickey for an advertising agency. Joe Heller, author of *Catch 22*, sold advertising for a magazine. Archibald MacLeish was Director of the Office of Facts and Figures during World War II. Stephen King was teaching high school English when he wrote *Carrie*. Pulitzer prize-winning novelist Jennifer Egan, author of *A Visit from the Goon Squad,* took a variety of odd jobs that allowed her time to write. For a while, she was the private secretary of the Countess of Romanones. And Charlotte Rogan, who published her first novel, *The Lifeboat,* in 2012 at age 57, after raising triplets and being a full-time housewife, spent 25 years writing in secret. Every author has had to find the time to write, and you can, too.

What makes a writer?

Novelist Kurt Vonnegut once remarked, "Talent is extremely common. What is rare is the willingness to endure the life of a writer. It is like making wallpaper by hand for the Sistine Chapel."

How does one know if he or she is a writer? Perhaps it is a single incident — one that happens early in life and shapes the writer's sense of wonder and self-awareness.

Take the case of José Saramago, the first Portuguese novelist to receive the Nobel Prize in Literature. The son of a peasant father and an illiterate mother, brought up in a home with no books, he took almost 40 years to go from metalworker to civil servant to production manager at a publishing house to newspaper editor. He was 60 before he earned recognition at home and abroad with *Baltasar and Blimunda*.

As a child he spent vacations with his grandparents in a village called Azinhaga. When his grandfather suffered a stroke and was to be taken to Lisbon for treatment, Saramago recalls, "He went into the yard of his house, where there were a few trees, fig trees, olive trees. And he went one by one, embracing the trees and crying, saying good-bye to them because he knew he would not return. To see this, to live this, if that doesn't mark you for the rest of your life, you have no feeling."

Begin with pure emotion and turn it into pure prose.

Let us begin

Sinclair Lewis was invited to talk to some students about the writer's craft. He stood at the head of the class and asked, "How many of you here are really serious about being writers?" A sea of hands shot up. Lewis then asked, "Well, why aren't you all home writing?" And with that he walked out of the room.

This book will entertain you, point you in the right direction and, most importantly, get you writing. For the purpose of organization, I am breaking your writing down into "days," but a "day" for you might be 30 minutes or it might be eight hours. Each day I will give you words of encouragement and advice, the wisdom of famous authors, and a task to do or questions to answer.

You must plan ahead. You may want to start writing your book at the beginning of summer when you have long days ahead of you, or at the start of a two-week vacation.

But first, you should sit down and read this short book in one sitting. Then begin again, and work through it, day by day, doing the exercises as you go along.

As you work — at your own pace — on the novel you always knew you could write, the only thing that matters is that you write something every day.

What you must do daily, besides writing, is track your progress by recording how many words you have written, and complete a short assignment that will help you organize your thoughts and stimulate your creativity. Don't worry. I'm an easy grader.

This is what you are going to do

Novelist Abigail Tarttelin, who sold her book *Golden Boy* to Orion Books in England for a six-figure advance in 2012 when she was in her early twenties, put it this way: "I'm not someone who doesn't have to earn money, so I've always had to wait tables while writing. It has never been easy for me to find space, time and energy to write, but I think it taught me that you have to use your time wisely. I come from a small town, I'm younger than most authors, I had no start up money and I knew no one in publishing. *Golden Boy* is living proof that hard work, support from a close circle of friends and family, taking risks and a lot of faith can produce a novel."

You can produce one.

I am going to teach you how, in the next 100 days.

The Beginning

DAY 1

On this first day, decide on the story you're going to write. You needn't have it worked out to every last detail, but today you are going to begin writing.

What is the book that you have always wanted to write? What type of novel appeals to you? What kind of story really gets your juices flowing? Is it a good murder mystery, science fiction, a thriller, romance or general fiction?

It doesn't matter what genre your novel is. There are no rules other than that the book must be interesting. It can be exciting, scary, fun, funny, romantic, sad or true down to the very last word. But it must not be boring.

How much time can you spend writing each day?

Be realistic about the amount of time you have to write. You don't have to write a lot every day. Ernest Hemingway wrote his first book, *The Sun Also Rises,* in seven weeks — that's approximately 1,500 words a day, but for most of his life he averaged 50 words a day when "the going was good."

Set a goal for yourself to write four pages a day. There are approximately 250 words on a page, so your goal is to write 1,000 words each day. Some days you'll only manage to produce one page, other days you may write 15 pages, but try to stick to your plan and average four pages a day.

If you maintain this routine, you will have a 240-page book at the end of the 60 days that are allotted for your writing of the first draft. Then you will spend the last 40 days editing, rewriting, reorganizing and writing some more.

Many publishing houses specify the format that submissions should follow (line spacing, font size, etc.). If you would like to format your pages properly from the start, see Day 92.

Okay, take a deep breath and start writing. Try for 1,000 words, but write whatever you can. Then do the exercise on the next page.

Today I wrote _____ *words.*

What is your favorite genre of novel? Why? Name some books in this genre that you enjoy.

What will be the genre of *your* novel? Why?

Describe your story in one sentence.

I always begin with a character, or characters, and then try and think up as much action for them as possible.

— John Irving
author of *The World According to Garp*

2 DAY

Choose your characters first as they are harder to imagine than the plot, and they are the keystone. As the legendary book editor Thomas McCormack writes,

> There's no doubt in my mind that the choice of the cast of characters is the most important decision the novelist makes, and that the choice cannot be optimally informed without attention to how they plug into one another, their circuitry.

As you write, your plot may or may not change, but your characters will develop and have a life of their own. As the characters develop, they'll take on distinct personalities, and, as with good friends, you will know in certain situations what they will or will not do.

Oakley Hall, mystery writer and author of *How Fiction Works,* says that a writer must "listen to the demands of his characters, who, as they begin to come to life, may insist upon a different fate than the givens seem to require."

Your characters will tell their own story, and if the story they tell surprises you, well, it will surprise the reader, too.

Today I wrote _____ *words.* _____

Write down the descriptions of your key characters.
You need to make these characters as familiar to you as the members
of your own family.

_____

_____

_____

_____

_____

_____

_____

_____

3
DAY

Without sounding overly sentimental about the process,
I'd say trying to describe how you tend to conceive of a
book is like describing how you tend to fall in love.

— Jess Walter
author of *Beautiful Ruins*

Carve a specific time out of your day to write. This is important because over the course of writing your novel, you'll get discouraged, bored, angry or otherwise fed up, and when you start feeling that way, you'll need a clearly defined routine to keep yourself going.

On occasion, you may need to shift your writing time to deal with other demands in your life, but keep to your regular schedule as much as you can.

What do I mean by specific writing time? For example: one hour each morning and two hours each evening, and one eight-hour day every weekend.

Decide how much time you will spend writing each week, and do it. Some would-be novelists defeat themselves because they set a schedule that is too difficult and they can't keep to it, so be realistic.

Today I wrote _____ *words.*

How much time can you devote to your writing every week?

_____

_____

When is the best time of day for you to write?

_____

_____

What is the best environment for you to write in?

_____

_____

DAY 4

Tell yourself you're going to set aside five minutes a day to write. If you can't do more, don't worry. But never let a day go by without doing your five minutes.

— Julie Myerson
author of *Something Might Happen*

You might like to try writing first in longhand, and then enter your work into the computer. This will give you two opportunities to think about what you have written before you start editing.

If you're finding it hard to write Chapter One, then begin by writing something about the place or the people in your book. It can be a lot easier to get started if you are writing about things with which you are already familiar.

Today I wrote _____ *words.* _____

Describe your main character — appearance, personality, history.

Describe the opening location of your story.

**DAY**

I sit here religiously every morning — I sit down for eight hours every day — and the sitting down is all. In the course of that working day of eight hours I write three sentences which I erase before leaving the table in despair . . . . Sometimes it takes all my resolution and power of self-control to refrain from butting my head against the wall.

— Joseph Conrad
author of *Heart of Darkness*

As an aspiring novelist you may already be jotting down descriptions of people you've observed, scenes you've imagined, and events you've experienced. If you have, pin each page separately to your office wall, or file them in a folder. If you haven't taken any such notes, begin to do so now.

What you will soon learn is that once you have written something down it is much easier to rewrite and expand on that, and see how it may fit into the larger picture — your novel. Always remember that nothing is wasted for the writer. He or she can use anything, and everything is of value, regardless of how small or unimportant it was at the time. It could become the key to your story.

Today I wrote _____ *words.* _____

Write about something with which you are very familiar — a person, a
place, a significant event — that you want to fictionalize in your novel.
Describe it in depth.

The complete novelist . . . would own the concentration of a Trappist monk, the organizational ability of a Prussian field marshal, the insights into human relations of a Viennese psychiatrist, the discipline of a man who prints the Lord's Prayer on the head of a pin, the exquisite sense of timing of an Olympic gymnast, and by the way, a natural instinct and flair for exceptional use of language.

— Leon Uris
author of *Exodus*

Rebecca Makkai said that when she was writing her novel *The Borrower*, "I found myself scouring my manuscript to remember, for the fifth time, whether I'd made that driveway gravel or paved, and where exactly it forked, and how long it was . . . . And so, 200 pages into my manuscript, I sat down to do what I should have done the first day . . . . For the first time in 20 years, I broke out the graph paper. I borrowed my daughter's colored pencils and sketched things out. Not just the general shape of the house, but 30 rooms plus couches, doors, rugs, the dog's water bowl, the junk in the attic. And since my novel is set in three time periods — the 1920s, '50s and '90s — at the same estate, I did all of this three times over."

She said the next time she sat down to write, "I did not mention the kitchen's square footage or that its stairs lay in the northeast corner. But I could say with utter confidence that my character ran up the kitchen stairs . . . . And if all this extra work is ridiculous, then so is fiction itself. What else do writers do, all day long, but try to convince the world that our imaginary castles are real? That our dream spaces belong to our readers too?"

Today I wrote _____ *words.* _____

Borrowing from Rebecca Makkai, sketch out the physical environment
of your book, whether it is a room, a house or a town, on a large piece
of paper and pin it to the wall so you have a handy visible reference to
the world you are creating.

Add notes to your sketch with new details as your novel develops.

DAY 7

Today make a promise to yourself that you are really going to write your novel. This is critical. Without that commitment, your book will never get written. Remember, you must write as often as you can. That's what writers do — they write.

You are not going to procrastinate. Procrastination is the writer's worst enemy, which you probably already know. After all, you've had that little voice in your head urging you to get started all these years. Henri Matisse advised his students, "If you want to be a painter, cut out your tongue." In other words, talking about your work will keep you from doing it.

Short story writer and novelist Yuvi Zalkow thinks it takes an aspiring author 10,000 hours of writing to master the craft. I disagree because I feel that no one has really mastered the craft of writing a novel. All novels fail in one way or another.

Today I wrote _____ *words.*

What is the working title of your novel?

_____

_____

_____

_____

_____

_____

_____

I don't believe that any writer can put in more than three hours' imaginative work a day.

— Philip Hensher
author of *King of the Badgers* and *Scenes from Early Life*

Writers write in different ways. Many write on computers, some in longhand, a few still use typewriters.

But it doesn't matter how you write. What matters is that you write. What you need to do in these 100 days is create a routine. Set your time and place to write.

Set up a studio in the place where you will usually write. Hopefully you can have a pin board nearby on which to hang your ideas. And keep this book nearby so that you can pencil in how many words you write each day.

You can write anywhere

You should carry a notepad with you at all times — you will be amazed at the places you can jot down a couple of sentences that come to you. If you are waiting for a meeting to begin, start writing. If you're on an airplane, start writing. If you are waiting for someone, write. Whenever there's a second, write. A few words, a thought, a sentence or two, they all count. Once written down, the words belong to you.

Today I wrote _____ *words.*

How did you spend your free time today?

_____

_____

_____

_____

List the locations where you wrote today.

_____

_____

_____

_____

DAY 9

Cram your head with characters and stories. Abuse your library privileges. Never stop looking at the world, and never stop reading to find out what sense other people have made of it. If people give you a hard time and tell you to get your nose out of a book, tell them you're working. Tell them it's research. Tell them to pipe down and leave you alone.

— Jennifer Weiner
author of *Good in Bed*

Here is a story from a friend of mine, Ralph Keyes, who wrote the wonderful book *The Courage to Write*.

Ralph tells of receiving an early morning phone call from a friend who had quit working at an insurance company to become a writer.

After a few days at her new profession, this friend called Ralph to get some pointers about her new career:

"You've been writing for a few years, right?" she began.

"Right," Ralph answered.

"Well, I have a very important question to ask you."

"Yes?"

"Do you get dressed in the morning or what?"

My answer — yes. It is important to get dressed, to treat writing as a serious task, not something that can be done while you are doing something else. Writing takes concentration and thought and dedication. So approach your prose as you might approach an important person. It deserves your respect and attention.

Today I wrote _____ *words.*

What do you do each day to get into the mindset to write?

_____

_____

_____

_____

_____

_____

_____

_____

DAY 10

I am a great believer in having the last line or last paragraph of my novel in mind before I start. I don't know exactly how I'll get there, but I have a destination.

Short story writer Katherine Anne Porter put it this way: "If I didn't know the ending of a story, I wouldn't begin. I always write my last line, my last paragraph, my last page first." She wrote the last page of *Ship of Fools* 20 years before she finished the novel.

Today I wrote _____ *words.*

Write down your first draft of the last line of your novel. Refer to it often.

**DAY**

11

Any clown with a sharp pencil can write out a dozen lines of verse and call them a poem. Not just any clown can fill 200 pages with prose and call it a book. Only the more determined clowns can get that job done.

— Lawrence Block
author of *The Thief Who Couldn't Sleep*

Ballet dancers know that they are going to have bloody feet. Pianists know that they'll have to practice until the pain in their fingers makes them cry.

Writers must realize that it is emotionally costly to write well. Writing a novel is mentally exhausting, far harder than working for someone else from nine to five. When you write a novel, you live the lives of your characters. Even when you are not writing, you are writing.

In the next three months, you will be living the secret life of the prose writer. You will be dreaming up plots and characters and situations, and you will be tempted to share these ideas with others. Don't. Keep your novel to yourself until it is on the printed page.

Today I wrote _____ *words.*

How do you feel when you're writing: Exhausted? Stressed? Happy?
All of these?

_____

_____

_____

_____

How do you feel after you are finished?

_____

_____

_____

_____

DAY 12

10 Steps to Becoming a Better Writer:

1. Write.
2. Write more.
3. Write even more.
4. Write even more than that.
5. Write when you don't want to.
6. Write when you do.
7. Write when you have something to say.
8. Write when you don't.
9. Write every day.
10. Keep writing.

— Brian Clark
on *CopyBlogger.com*

In the spirit of Brian Clark, whom I've quoted above, here are six practices that will help you finish your novel.

- Write at the same time every day.
- Never wait until you "feel like writing."
- Turn off all distractions, like email or the evening news.
- Set a goal to write a minimum number of words each day.
- Don't try to write too much.
- Try this trick of Ernest Hemingway's: End each session in mid-sentence or mid-paragraph so that you'll have an easier time starting up the next day.

Today I wrote _____ *words.*

List the steps — or practices — that you plan to follow to do a good
day's work every day on your book.

The Characters

DAY **13**

> You can never know enough about your characters.
>
> — W. Somerset Maugham
> author of *The Razor's Edge*

Get a batch of 4" x 6" index cards and write each character's name at the top of a card.

Next, think about the role each character plays in your story, and what kind of person each is: age, education, place of birth, appearance, mannerisms, personality. Are they shy, hotheaded, funny, squirrelly? What are their quirks? Do they wash their hands 500 times a day? Do they hear voices? Are they kind to kids, but love to torture cats? Write it all down on the character's card. Put down so much that you finally come to know these characters intimately.

Some characters will be major ones driving the action of the story; others will play only bit parts. Regardless, the details of their personalities and lives are critical to adding interest to your story.

You must remember, however, that every character must have a reason for being. If they do not, they will slow the book down and, worst of all, bore the reader.

Using this same index-card technique, film director and producer Alfred Hitchcock would write down information about each scene of his next film, one scene to a card. By the time he was ready to shoot, he had a completely developed story — and a very tight one at that.

Today I wrote _____ *words.*

To give yourself a comfort level with the material that you are creating,
list what was happening in the world during the time frame of your novel.

_____

_____

_____

Now list the name and age of each of your characters, and how the
events of the time might mold his or her thoughts and actions.

_____

_____

_____

_____

_____

14 DAY

If a writer is true to his characters, they will give him his plot.

— Phyllis Bottome
author of *Private Worlds*

The reader has to believe that your characters exist or could exist, and they need to be distinctively drawn. Nothing better defines characters than their actions, their purpose in life. Their purpose may be good or evil. It doesn't matter. All that matters is that the reader sees their actions and purpose, believes them, and continues to be interested in them.

Do not create a cast of thousands. Write a tale about two or three memorable characters, all of them filled with purpose.

Today I wrote _____ _words._

List your main characters.

List your minor characters.

How many characters are in your novel?
(Unless you are Charles Dickens, 50 is too many.)

DAY 15

Writing is a job, a talent, but it's also the place to go in your head. It is the imaginary friend you drink your tea with in the afternoon.

— Ann Patchett
author of *Truth and Beauty*

Your novel can be light on plot and short on style, but if your characters are real they can save your book by gaining the reader's sympathy.

Keep your characters "in character" in terms of what they are wearing, how they speak, their traits, their dialogue, their behavior, their motivations. In doing so, over the pages of your book, your characters will become flesh and blood to the reader.

Today I wrote _____ *words.*

List the characters you remember best from novels you've read. What
made them real and interesting to you?

DAY 16

To imagine yourself inside another person . . . is what a storywriter does in every piece of work; it is his first step, and his last too, I suppose.

— Eudora Welty
author of *The Optimist's Daughter*

You need a strong protagonist, someone who draws the reader into the story.

This is the person with whom your reader will identify. You want your reader to care about your protagonist.

You may have a main character who is a villain, but he or she is not the protagonist of your story. The protagonist is the hero or heroine who will carry the narrative to the climax of the novel.

Today I wrote _____ *words.*

List as much information as you can about your protagonist. Express
the information as if you were writing to a friend about someone you
met and found fascinating.

DAY 17

It took me fifteen years to discover I had no talent for writing, but I couldn't give it up because by that time I was too famous.

— Robert Benchley
author of *The Best of Robert Benchley*

It is time to give your protagonist a name.

Names are important. Serious thought should go into this decision — the name should suggest the type of person you are writing about. For example, a librarian should not be named Alexa or Valerie; a glamorous woman shouldn't be called Mary or Ruth.

Each name must also fit the time period of your novel. Names go in and out of fashion. For example, the name Sadie was popular in the early 20th century and is again now, but you most likely would not have heard of a young woman named Sadie in the 1960s or '70s.

Today I wrote _____ *words.* _____

List some names that you like for your protagonist. You don't have to make a choice now. The right name will come to you as you continue your story and the character becomes more real.

18 DAY

I can tell a story in the third person or in the first person, and perhaps in the second person singular, or in the first person plural, though successful examples of these latter two are rare indeed. And that is it. Anything else probably will not much resemble narration; it may be closer to poetry, or prose-poetry.

— James Wood
author of *How Fiction Works*

"Point of view" is a term that refers to the relationships between the storyteller, the story and the reader. A story can be told from three different points of view — first person, second person or third person.

Many writers' natural inclination is to have a narrator who tells his or her own story in the first person. Think of J. D. Salinger's *The Catcher in the Rye*. A first-person storyteller can also tell someone else's story, as did Nick Carraway in F. Scott Fitzgerald's *The Great Gatsby*.

Other writers use the third-person point of view. There are various kinds of third-person narrators. Two examples are:

- An *omniscient storyteller* who goes everywhere, knows everything, reveals what is in the minds of the characters, and comments when he or she wants. For a good example of this technique look at Mary Gordon's novel, *The Other Side*.

- A *direct observer* who has no memory of the past, and no special understanding of the present. The direct observer is like a reporter in the room recording the scene. This point of view is best used for a story that is all action and dialogue. For good examples, look at almost any of Hemingway's novels.

Some stories are told in the second person "you" — like Jay McInerney's *Bright Lights, Big City* — but the use of second-person is rare.

Today I wrote _____ *words.* _____

From what point of view is the story told in your favorite novel?

How did that point of view enhance the telling of the story?

DAY 19

> Times are bad. Children no longer obey their parents and everyone is writing a book.
>
> — Cicero, circa 43 BC

There are other points of view that can be used to tell a story, but for purposes of your first novel, let's keep it simple.

You should decide to use either the first person or the third-person omniscient where the author — you — knows everything about all the characters, including all their emotions and thoughts. Try to rewrite the opening of your novel from a point of view different from the one you have chosen, and see how it reads. What feels better for you to tell your story? Go with your feelings.

You can get creative with points of view on your next book, but let's write this one first.

Today I wrote _____ *words.* _____

Which of the two recommended points of view do you choose for your novel?

Write a few sentences of your story using this point of view.

Now write the same sentences from the other point of view.

Which point of view feels more comfortable for you? Why?

I did not begin to write novels until I had forgotten all I had learned at school and college.

— John Galsworthy
author of *The Forsyte Saga*

Commit yourself to the point of view early in your planning and stay with it. This enables you — and the reader — to get a footing in the story.

In your novel, you might have more than one point of view. In my family saga novel, *Brothers & Sisters*, there were six children and each one told his or her story. I introduced them all in the first chapter with individual scenes, and, therefore, the reader understood immediately how I was telling the story. This technique also allowed me to handle comfortably a large cast of characters.

Today I wrote _____ *words.* _____

Which character will be your viewpoint character?

Why?

Every writer I know has trouble writing.

— Virginia Woolf
author of *A Room of One's Own*

Keep asking the question, "Why?"

Why did your character take a different route to work that day? Why did she avoid his kiss? Why did they decide to eat at home Friday evening? Why did she go to Africa? Why doesn't he like to fly?

A novel in many ways imitates life, reflects life, and tells the story of our lives, yet novels are different from real life. By that I mean that our days are filled with unconnected and random actions and events. In a novel, everything matters, and the actions of your characters must have meaning, even if the reader doesn't know the significance of an utterance, gesture or life decision at the time it happens.

Today I wrote _____ *words.* _____

For each of the characters in your novel, write down one important
detail about him or her that will have an impact on the plot.

DAY 22

An author in his book must be like God in the universe, present everywhere and visible nowhere.

— Gustave Flaubert
author of *Madame Bovary*

Figure out what your characters need to do in your story, what they do together, what they do to one another and what the story does to them.

You must decide: Are they all pulling together in one direction? Or are they pulling in six different directions?

To help you decide, always ask yourself these critical questions: Which option would be most interesting to the reader? Will the reader care? These questions are the real litmus test of character development and plotting. To be successful, you need to make hard choices. You need to be ruthless with your characters and your story. Who's in, who's out? What's in, what's out?

Frankly, this is where a lot of first-time novelists fail. They can't bring themselves to choose. They become fascinated or paralyzed by the possibilities.

Don't do that. Be brutal.

Try different choices, of course, but move the story forward, event by event, bringing each character along with you. As each event unfolds, each character must react to it just as he or she would in real life.

If a child is hit by a car and killed, the driver's life is changed forever, as are the lives of the child's parents and his brothers and sisters, friends, even the crossing guard and bystanders. You have to decide what the changes are. This is your chance to play God — and if you're going to write, you must play that role.

Today I wrote _____ *words.* _____

What are some of the choices you must make in regard to your
characters?

_____

_____

_____

_____

_____

_____

_____

_____

The Plot

23 DAY

Writing a novel is like driving a car at night. You can only see as far as your headlights, but you can make the whole trip that way.

— E. L. Doctorow
author of *Ragtime*

You should now begin to develop your characters and your plot together. You can't do one well without the other. Your characters are not wooden people who just dropped out of the sky. They are critical elements of the drama you are creating. They must do something logical or illogical (which is what plot is all about) that adds to your story, and moves it to its climax. Never separate characters from plot.

Today I wrote _____ *words.* _____

Summarize what will happen in your next few chapters. This will force
you to develop the plot.

**DAY 24**

> Caress the detail, the divine detail. Details make stories human, and the more human a story can be, the better.
>
> — Vladimir Nabokov
> author of *Lolita*

Good characters grow and evolve out of basically two things: their actions and their outlook on life. Readers develop an understanding of the characters by what they do and think in the dramatic events of the story.

As the plot progresses, so should your characters' development. Pay attention to traits or ticks they display, the clothes they wear, and how they respond to situations. Remember to add these enhancements to your characters' index cards to maintain consistency.

Today I wrote _____ *words.*

In developing your characters, are you paying attention to both their
actions and their beliefs? Give an example.

 **DAY**

I think what I love most [about writing] is that feeling that you really nailed something. I rarely feel it with a whole piece, but sometimes with a line you feel that it really captured what it is that you had inside you and you got it out for a stranger to read, someone who may never love you or meet you, but he or she is going to get that experience from that line.

— Andre Dubus III
author of *Townie — A Memoir*

Characters do not operate in a vacuum. Their actions usually involve other people, and these interactions are what make up scenes. A single scene or a telling description can be a building block for constructing a unified story line.

Today I wrote _____ *words.* _____

What is the essence of your central characters? Try to express each
character's essence in two to three sentences.

DAY 26

When I sit at my table to write, I never know what it's going to be till I'm underway. I trust in inspiration, which sometimes comes and sometimes doesn't. But I don't sit back waiting for it. I work every day.

— Alberto Moravia
author of *La Noia*

Although there are no rules about story ideas, I would offer you one caution: Think small. One of the worst mistakes most beginning novelists make is thinking big, trying to come up with an end-of-the-world story in the belief that big is better. That's not true. Even if your plot is "big," make the characters "small," as in detailed and well crafted.

Look into your creative soul and search for a little story, yet one that has real meaning to you. We are all part of the human family. If you create a story that has deep meaning to you, chances are it will have deep meaning for the rest of us.

Alice Munro is considered by many to be the best short-story writer in the English language. Her books sell about 30,000 copies a year. She is a writer other writers admire for her technical skills and the purity of her style.

She is also known for the complex structure of her stories. But what is most interesting about Alice Munro — who lives in a small town in southern Canada — is that her stories are about ordinary people: their secrets, their memories, their acts of violence, their sexual longings.

Even if your novel is about the paranormal — another *Blade Runner* or *The Adjustment Bureau* — draw your characters with common, human traits that you observe every day in the people you know.

Today I wrote _____ *words.*

Does your story have meaning beyond action and plot?

Describe it in one sentence.

**DAY**

The cat sat on the mat is not a story. The cat sat on the other cat's mat is a story.

— John le Carré
author of *The Spy Who Came in from the Cold*

I have written twelve novels in three distinct genres. To prepare myself for writing these novels, I researched and read classics and famous novels in each of these genres.

To write my horror/occult novels, I read everything that was written by Stephen King and Peter Straub. I read the short stories of Edgar Allan Poe, Harlan Ellison, Lawrence Block, Ray Bradbury, Robert Bloch and dozens of others who have written short stories and novels in this genre. I was studying how *they* did it.

When writing my family saga, I went to multi-generational books and analyzed the patterns within that form. I looked at the way writers in the genre handled the narratives of long, multi-plotted generational novels.

I turned to writers who used golf as a subject of their fiction when beginning to write my three novels that had country club life as the environment and a caddie as the protagonist. I read the short stories that featured a caddie written by Ernest Hargreaves, John Updike, John P. Marquand, Michael Murphy, J. Michael Vernon, and, of course, Steven Pressfield, who wrote the *The Legend of Bagger Vance*.

I researched the history of the game of golf, as well as golf course design, and the ambiance of country club life. I felt comfortable from my own experience as a caddie to create the atmosphere of the caddie yard. All that was left was the plot.

I had analyzed. I had learned. I was prepared to then create a readable story.

Today I wrote _____ *words.*

Read your favorite novel again as if it were a how-to manual, and outline the action on large sheets of paper and pin the sheets to your office wall. Answer these questions:

- What is the genre of the novel?

- What is the average length of each chapter?

- Who is the central character?

- What is the point of view?

- What does the author do on the first page or in the first chapter to gain your interest and attention?

- What is it about the novel that keeps you reading?

Now think about *your* book. Write down your ideas on paper so that you can go back to them later if you need them.

- Analyze the plot, and compare it to the plot of your favorite novel. What is lacking in your book that needs to be fixed?

- What new twist can you come up with that will make your novel more interesting and exciting?

- What have you learned about plot development from doing this exercise?

DAY 28

Every fine story must leave in the mind of the sensitive reader an intangible residuum of pleasure, a cadence, a quality of voice that is exclusively the writer's own, individual, unique.

— Willa Cather
author of *Death Comes for the Archbishop*

Imitation can lead to originality.

Do short exercises imitating different styles. Try on a dozen different voices in your prose until you find one you like. Ape the sure hand of a master. But remember this: Borrow a style, but write from your own experience. Your experience is unique.

John Braine, author of *Room at the Top*, wrote, "If you're to be heard out of all those thousands of voices, if your name is going to mean something out of all those thousands of names, it will only be because you've presented your own experience truthfully."

Today I wrote _____ *words.*

As a writer, what voice works best for you?

_____

_____

Write down a sentence or two to illustrate your voice.

_____

_____

_____

_____

_____

Look at the novel you are writing. Is it written in your best voice?

_____

_____

I start at the beginning, go on to the end, then stop.

— Anthony Burgess
author of *A Clockwork Orange*

DAY 29

When I was writing my first published novel, *The Piercing*, I imposed a structure on the plot that complemented the religious overtones of the book. As a specific time frame for my story I chose the 40 days of Lent. I then divided the book into 40 chapters, one for each day. This structure enabled me to pace the story while always having an overview of where it was going.

Today I wrote _____ *words.* _____

Chart a timeline that lays out the structure of days, months or years
during which your book will take place.

DAY 30

I have advice for people who want to write. . . . First, you need to keep an honest, unpublishable journal that nobody reads, nobody but you. . . . Second, you need to read. You can't be a writer if you're not a reader. The third thing is to write. Just write a little bit every day. Even if it's for only half an hour — write, write, write.

— Madeleine L'Engle
author of *A Wrinkle in Time*

By now you should be about halfway through the first draft of your novel. If you have written four pages a day (with approximately 250 words per page) for the last 30 days, you have written about 30,000 words. If you keep up this pace, once you have completed your first draft you will have plenty of time to edit and rewrite — and edit and rewrite again.

But if you have written 10,000 words, not 30,000, don't worry. Writers work at different paces. Keep going. Keep *your* pace. Write down how many words you have written and turn the page. Continue. You are doing great. You are still writing.

Today I wrote _____ *words.* _____

How many words have you written since Day One? _____

_____

_____

_____

_____

_____

_____

_____

DAY

It is not a good idea to try to put your wife into a novel
. . . not your latest wife anyway.

— Norman Mailer
author of *The Naked and the Dead*

Some action-driven novels — especially big commercial books — follow a plot formula.

For example, John Baldwin, who coauthored *The Eleventh Plague: A Novel of Medical Terror* with John S. Marr, developed a 10-step formula:

1. The hero is an expert.
2. The villain is an expert.
3. You must watch all of the villainy over the shoulder of the villain.
4. The hero has a team of experts in various fields behind him.
5. Two or more on the team must fall in love.
6. Two or more on the team must die.
7. The villain must turn his attention from his initial goal to the team.
8. The villain and the hero must live to do battle again in a sequel.
9. All deaths must proceed from the individual to the group. For example, never say "The bomb exploded and 15,000 people were killed." Start with, "Jamie and Suzy were walking in the park with their grandmother when the earth opened up."
10. If you get bogged down, just kill somebody.

Does this sound ridiculous to you? Perhaps so — but think of your favorite suspense novels and see if at least some of this formula doesn't apply.

Today I wrote _____ *words.*

If you are writing an action-driven novel, what is your formula? (If your book is not an action story, skip this assignment.)

DAY 32

I base my characters partly on the people I know — one can't escape it — but fictional characters are over-simplified; they're much less complex than the people one knows.

— Aldous Huxley
author of *Brave New World*

If John Baldwin's formula isn't for you, you might consider Ernest Hemingway's approach. When he started as a young reporter for the *Kansas City Star*, he was given a style sheet with four basic rules:

- Use short sentences.
- Use short first paragraphs.
- Use vigorous English.
- Be positive, never negative.

Years later, he said, "Those were the best rules I ever learned in the business of writing. I've never forgotten them. No one with any talent, who feels and writes truly about the things he is trying to say, can fail to write well if he abides by them."

Today I wrote _____ *words.* _____

If you don't like John Baldwin's 10-step formula, what four basic rules would suit you?

_____

_____

_____

_____

_____

_____

_____

_____

DAY **33**

Beginning a book is unpleasant. I'm entirely uncertain about the character and the predicament, and a character in his predicament is what I have to begin with. . . . I type out beginnings and they're awful, more of an unconscious parody of my previous book than the breakaway from it that I want. I need something driving down the center of a book, a magnet to draw everything to it — that's what I look for during the first months of writing something new.

— Philip Roth
author of *Goodbye, Columbus*

Don't be afraid to write down scenes or sections that don't lead anywhere. And don't discard them if you can't use them at the moment.

Joan Didion once said that she pins her ideas on a board in the hope of using them later and she gave this example: Quite early in the writing of her novel *A Book of Common Prayer*, she wrote about one of the central characters going to the airport. It was a couple of pages of prose that she liked, but she couldn't find a place for it. "I kept picking this part up and putting it in different places, but it kept stopping the narrative; it was wrong everywhere, but I was determined to use it." She finally found a spot for it. "Sometimes you can get away with things in the middle of the book," she said.

Today I wrote _____ *words.*

Do you have a favorite scene for which you can't find a "place" in your novel? Write it here.

_____

_____

_____

Why do you like it?

_____

_____

_____

_____

_____

DAY 34

We've got to get one more "Will he? Won't he?" into this.

— William Wyler
Film Director
while making the movie *Friendly Persuasion*

Rent the film *Friendly Persuasion*, and note how director William Wyler created that "Will he? Won't he?" tension. Then read Jessamyn West's novel *The Friendly Persuasion*, and see how it lacks those moments. If you can't find the movie, get the recent film *Salmon Fishing in the Yemen* and see how the director created tensions with shifts in the story line.

If you are having trouble creating plot tension, just write individual scenes with your characters and don't worry about fitting them into a narrative. That can come later in the rewriting of your novel.

Today I wrote _____ *words.*

Write down examples of how plot shifts create tension in the movies
Friendly Persuasion and *Salmon Fishing in the Yemen.*

 **DAY**

The invention of movable type created opportunities for writers that could barely be imagined in Gutenberg's day. The opportunities that await writers in the near future are immeasurably greater.

— Jason Epstein
former editor in chief of Random House

Rick Bass, one of America's finest stylists, says that a fiction writer — like a mason — needs both power and precision to construct a good story. As he puts it, "You've got to lay the stones one on top of the other so they fit together, but you've got to have the strength to lug them around."

Bonnie Jo Campbell, another fine literary writer and author of *Once Upon a River* and other books, explains the development of a novel this way:

> In most novels, any given scene is proportionally a small bit of the story, and yet the scene still needs to reflect all that's essential about the novel, must acknowledge the scenes that came before and lay groundwork for what comes after, while, hopefully, being compelling in its own right. To be honest, I don't know how anybody writes a novel.

Today I wrote _____ *words.* _____

What "stones" are you using to build your story? Do they fit together?

_____

_____

_____

_____

_____

_____

_____

_____

DAY 36

On the whole, I don't want to think too much about why I write what I write. If I know what I'm doing . . . I can't do it.

— Joan Didion
author of *Slouching Towards Bethlehem*

The chapters of a novel need to gain momentum and each chapter needs to be "larger" than the previous one.

Think of your chapters as rooms in a building in which each space that one enters is larger than the previous one, and you, as the author, are leading a tour. The readers must sense that as they read they are making progress: learning, and understanding more and more about the characters and the situation.

Today I wrote _____ *words.*

Draw a diagram of progressively larger squares and label them to demonstrate how your plot is growing in intensity, complexity or suspense.

37 DAY

It is necessary to write, if the days are not to slip emptily by. How else, indeed, to clap the net over the butterfly of the moment? For the moment passes, it is forgotten; the mood is gone; life itself is gone. That is where the writer scores over his fellows: He catches the changes of his mind on the hop.

— Vita Sackville-West
author of *All Passion Spent*

Shirley Jackson, as the mother of four children and wife of a college professor, rarely had time to write during the day. Yet when she sat down at her desk at night, a story like "The Lottery" flowed out in a perfect first draft.

Why? Because she had been thinking about her story all day.

Agatha Christie said that the best time to plan a book is while doing the dishes.

Count on your subconscious to take charge and work through ideas that come to you during the day.

Many authors have noticed this phenomenon. Novelist Tony D'Souza calls it "writing off the page."

Today I wrote _____ *words.* _____

What did you "write off the page" today? ....

DAY 38

> Write the kind of story you would like to read. People will give you all sorts of advice about writing, but if you are not writing something you like, no one else will like it either.
>
> — Meg Cabot
> author of *The Princess Diaries*

Before we leave the problem of finding your story, let me debunk another cliché about novel writing: Write only about something you know.

You've heard that before. It's nonsense. Tom Clancy had never been a submarine commander before he wrote *The Hunt for Red October*. And it's a safe bet that Richard Bach had never been a seagull before he wrote *Jonathan Livingston Seagull*.

Instead of writing about something that you know, you can write about something that you find compelling and want to know more about.

Arthur Golden, author of *Memoirs of a Geisha*, was living in Tokyo and working for an English-language magazine when, in 1982, he had the idea for the novel.

Upon returning to the U.S. he earned a creative writing degree from Boston University, and then in 1986 began researching geishas and discovered "a subculture with its own strange rules." It took him 10 years and several drafts before he sold the book to Alfred A. Knopf for $250,000.

Today I wrote _____ *words.*

Make a list of things that you want to use in your novel that will require you to do extensive research. Note when and how you will do that research.

39

Nobody reads a mystery to get to the middle. They read it to get to the end. If it's a letdown, they won't buy any more. The first page sells that book. The last page sells your next book.

— Mickey Spillane
author of *I, the Jury*

Suspense is a basic ingredient of all writing. Because of it, readers wonder what is going to happen next, and they will keep reading to find out. Jackie Collins, author of *Hollywood Wives* and many other best sellers, is a master of this technique. So, make something happen at the end of each chapter that will make your readers want more.

In my suspense novels, I try to create a situation where my characters are backed into a corner at the end of a chapter so that the reader wants to immediately start the next chapter to see what happens.

Today I wrote _____ *words.*

List some ways to build suspense in your novel. It could be something simple, such as a telephone ringing in a dark house and no one
answering when the character says "hello."

The Details

DAY 40

For me, a good thriller must teach me something about the real world. Thrillers like *Coma*, *The Hunt for Red October* and *The Firm* all captivated me by providing glimpses into realms about which I knew very little — medical science, submarine technology and the law. To my taste, a great thriller must also contain at its core a thought-provoking ethical debate or moral dilemma.

— Dan Brown
author of *The Da Vinci Code*

What I strive to do is write novels of information. I want readers to come away from my books having learned something new while also having enjoyed a compelling story.

Yet the challenge for the writer is not to burden readers with details but to share with them fascinating stories that are informed by solid research.

Remember, small pieces go a long way. Don't drown your novel in information.

Today I wrote _____ *words.*

Describe three interesting facts that help form the background of your plot.

_____

_____

_____

_____

_____

_____

_____

_____

41
DAY

Your novel is a work of fiction, but that doesn't mean your facts don't need to be straight.

Nothing turns a reader off quite as fast as a recognizable inaccuracy. And nothing gives a story the ring of authenticity like the right fact or detail.

Use the Internet for research. It's fast, easy and inexpensive. Every library in the world is open to you. However, the Internet is not a totally reliable source, so be sure to have two sources for every piece of essential information.

Look, too, at magazines and newspapers published at the same time and place as the setting of your novel. Gore Vidal used old editions of *Harper's* magazine for details when writing some of his historical novels.

Today I wrote _____ *words.*

Record the source of every bit of information that you have obtained through research. You will need this list later when you fact-check your novel.

42 DAY

If you're going to be a writer, you first of all have to develop unusual powers of observation . . . of other people. . . . I was always an eager eavesdropper, and I still am. . . . You have to have an ear for the way different people speak, for the way they express themselves, for the pauses that indicate what is not being said. That sort of instinct is something that a writer subconsciously begins to teach herself.

— Nadine Gordimer
author of *Burger's Daughter*

Conversation is not dialogue.

Dialogue has a purpose. It pushes the story forward. It keeps the reader tuned in to the story, and makes him or her feel at the heart of the action. Put the reader in the middle of your story's action and your dialogue will sing naturally. Keep your talk efficient and forceful.

It is important to always make certain that the reader knows who is speaking. In many situations, given the flow of the dialogue, you will be able to eliminate many of the "he said"/"she said" attributions that slow down the story.

Try to build something into the dialogue that indirectly tells the reader who is speaking. For example, besides "he said," you might have a line that reads:

"We'll never escape alive." He flicked his cigarette away in disgust.

Today I wrote _____ *words.*

Look at one of your pages of dialogue. How many times have you written "he said" or "she said" on that page?

Try rewriting that dialogue to eliminate these attributions.

You never have to change anything you got up in the middle of the night to write.

— Saul Bellow
author of *Henderson the Rain King*

The narrative of a novel moves most successfully with dialogue. You can get a lot of information out to a reader with a few lines. Nevertheless, your chapters can become too "talky," and conveying too much information through dialogue can mean more "telling" than "showing."

Consider moving your story forward with simple summary paragraphs that describe a situation and push the plot along.

Here is an example from Hilary Mantel's *Wolf Hall*:

Next day he felt the gods at his back, like a breeze. He turned back toward Europe. Home then was a narrow shuttered house on a quiet canal, Anselma kneeling, creamily naked under her trailing nightgown of green damask, its sheen blackish in candlelight; kneeling before the small silver altarpiece she kept in her room, which was precious to her, she had told him, the most precious thing I own. Excuse me just a moment, she had said; she prayed in her own language, now coaxing, now almost threatening, and she must have teased from her silver saints some flicker of grace, or perceived some deflection in their glinting rectitude, because she stood up and turned to him, saying, "I'm ready now," tugging apart the silk tie of her gown so that he could take her breasts in his hands.

Today I wrote _____ *words.*

Locate a page (or less) of dialogue in your novel. Now sum it up below with one paragraph of narrative. You might be surprised to see that you can quickly move the story forward without losing tension or the story line.

**DAY**

What no spouse of a writer can ever understand is that a writer is working when he or she is staring out of a window.

— Burton Rascoe
author of *Titans of Literature*

Aim for one startling image on each page. For example, try to match this image of a sunrise at sea in *The Voyage* by Philip Caputo:

> A golden shimmer appeared where the horizon was supposed to be, then a red sun pushed up, like the head of some fiery infant bulging out of the gray sea's womb — water giving birth to its opposite element.

Today I wrote _____ *words.* _____

Write what you think is a startling image and keep it handy. You might
find a good spot for it — perhaps to open a new chapter.

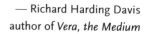
The secret of good writing is to say an old thing a new way or to say a new thing an old way.

— Richard Harding Davis
author of *Vera, the Medium*

Don't write 1,000 pages just because technology makes it easy for you to do it. The computer and the Internet make it tempting to over-research and over-write, but keep thinking small.

We all feel that movies and baseball games are too long. What about books? Publishers and editors will tell you: A story determines its own length. Remember that *The Great Gatsby* is considered by many to be the great American novel, and it is just 200 pages long.

Today I wrote _____ *words.*

What is the total number of words you have written? What percentage
of the novel will that comprise?

**46** DAY

A story isn't a charcoal sketch, where every stroke lies on the surface to be seen. It's an oil painting, filled with layers that the author must uncover so carefully to show its beauty.

— Amelia Atwater-Rhodes
author of *In the Forests of the Night*

Without descriptions, the reader doesn't have a sense of place, time and mood — all critical to your story. But with too much description, your novel will bog down and get boring. Give only the telling details. Create a world where your characters can live and breathe, and not drown.

Today I wrote _____ *words.* _____

Write down the best description you have written so far for this book.
I promise, it will cheer you up when you read it back to yourself.

**DAY 47**

Nice writing isn't enough. It isn't enough to have smooth and pretty language. You have to surprise the reader frequently, you can't just be nice all the time. Provoke the reader. Astonish the reader. Writing that has no surprises is as bland as oatmeal. Surprise the reader with the unexpected verb or adjective. Use one startling adjective per page.

— Anne Bernays
author of *Growing Up Rich*

Ideas, new and unique — they are what surprise, satisfy and please readers. Stay away from the tried and true. Write with imagination. If your images, metaphors, similes and expressions sound familiar, then they are. Think of better ones.

Today I wrote _____ *words.*

Write down all the "tried and true" expressions, metaphors, etc. that
you have used so far, cut them out, and keep that list so you won't be
tempted to use them again in this novel — or any other novel.

DAY 48

When I was writing my first novel, *The Art of Disappearing*, and things weren't going as well as I wished, I'd visit BookCourt, a bookstore around the corner from our house. I'd stand outside the store and look at the new releases in the window and imagine my book being one of them. I'd imagine high school classmates and teachers noticing my name and buying my book. I'd hope that children picking out their summer reading, might one day select my novel.

— Ivy Pochoda
author of *Visitation Street*

Don't get discouraged. Keep writing.

The Pulitzer Prize-winning novel *Ironweed* by William Kennedy was rejected by 13 publishers before Saul Bellow intervened on its behalf.

A writer becomes a writer by writing. You have to put in the time to achieve what you want.

Today I wrote _____ *words.*

How much time are you allowing yourself to become a published writer?

_____

_____

_____

_____

_____

_____

_____

_____

If a gun hangs on the wall in the first act of the play, it must be discharged before the end.

— Anton Chekhov
author of *The Seagull*

You have to look at your total work with Anton Chekhov's remarkably simple piece of advice in mind, and cut out anything that doesn't help the story complete itself. Remember, every detail that you put into your novel should matter in terms of your plot.

Plots are built with small bricks of information until you've completed the whole building.

Today I wrote _____ *words.*

What are your "guns on the wall"?

DAY 50

Pedestrian writing, thin characters — I can handle the criticism. I write to pedestrians. And I am a pedestrian. I write the best I can. I know I'm never going to be revered as some classic writer. I don't claim to be C. S. Lewis. The literary-type writers, I admire them. I wish I was smart enough to write a book that's hard to read, you know?

— Jerry Jenkins
co-author of the *Left Behind* series

Another way to describe a character is with action. For example, in his short story "The Eighty-Yard Run" Irwin Shaw sets the whole story in motion:

> The pass was high and wide and he jumped for it, feeling it slap flatly against his hands, as he shook his hips to throw off the halfback who was diving at him.
>
> The center floated by, his hands desperately brushing Darling's knee as Darling picked his feet up high and delicately ran over a blocker and an opposing linesman in a jumble on the ground near the scrimmage line. He had ten yards in the clear and picked up speed, breathing easily, feeling his thigh pads rising and falling against his legs, listening to the sound of cleats behind him, pulling away from them, watching the other backs heading him off toward the sideline, the whole picture, the man closing in on him, the blockers' fights for position, the ground he had to cross all suddenly clear in his head, for the first time in his life not a meaningless confusion of men, sounds, speed.

Today I wrote _____ *words.*

Review what you have written so far and see if you can add a description
of body language that will convey something about a character as well
as hint at what is coming later.

51

I wrote for a long time purely for myself. The writing was my survival actually. It was my way of being with them. The more I wrote, the more real they became to me.

— Sonali Deraniyagala
author of Wave

Memoir of the December, 2004 Sri Lanka tsunami that she miraculously survived, but which killed her parents, husband and two young sons.

In 1979, at the age of 80, Jessie Lee Brown Foveaux began to write the story of her life. She wrote innocent tales of her past, tales of her grandmother, and of a distant Aunt Clara who chewed tobacco and could spit in a cat's eye.

Every morning she went into the kitchen of her white two-bedroom house in Manhattan, Kansas, where she had raised eight children. She sat down at the table and, aided by scrapbooks, letters and photographs, she wrote. Day after day, week after week, she wrote in longhand the story of her life, noting the watershed events: births, deaths, one marriage, three wars, one flood, as well as the things that just struck her fancy, like the first time she saw Lawrence Welk. Having covered the events of her life, she began to write about a world she'd never spoken of — her feelings and thoughts. Jessie Lee wrote all of this for her "Harvest of Age" senior citizen writing class taught by Charley Kempthorne.

Her writings were published by the local

college under the title *The Life of Jessie Lee Brown From Birth Up to 80 Years*. About 30 copies were printed for her family and friends.

In 1997 Mr. Kempthorne sent a copy of the book to the *Wall Street Journal*. What followed was a front-page article in the paper and an auction for the publishing rights. The book sold to Warner Books when Jessie Lee was 98 years old. It was published with the title *Any Given Day: The Life and Times of Jessie Lee Brown Foveaux*.

Jessie Lee contacted Mr. Kempthorne, the teacher who had encouraged her to tell her story: "Thank you so much for not giving up on me. I am not a writer, but my poor efforts have made a great difference in my life."

If Jessie Lee Brown Foveaux isn't a writer, who is? Her book isn't a novel, of course, but it tells a story — Jessie Lee's story. And Warner bought the publishing rights for one million dollars.

Today I wrote _____ *words.*

In one or two sentences, explain what writing your novel really means
to you. Why is it important for you to finish your book?

The long-lived books of tomorrow are concealed somewhere amongst the so-far unpublished MSS of today.

— Philip Unwin
in *The Publishing Unwins*

Go to the library and browse through books
on food and gardening. You'll see that the
authors describe smells, tastes, touches and
even sounds in precise detail. When writing,
always mention scents and tactile sensations.
Good description addresses all the senses.

Today I wrote _____ *words.*

List the titles of the food and gardening books that were helpful in this exercise — you may want to consult them again.

List some of the words that describe smells, sounds, textures, etc.

Verbs blast you down the highway.

— Rita Mae Brown
author of *Rubyfruit Jungle*

53 DAY

Select your details with care. You don't need a lot of them, but you need the right ones. As Mark Twain said: "Use the right word, not its second cousin." Remember, too, that verbs are the strongest parts of any sentence. Don't rely on easy ones like *is*, *have*, *go*, *got*, etc.

Today I wrote _____ *words.*

Rewrite a description in one of your scenes and see if you can make it
more vivid by focusing on good details and strong verbs.

Don't tell me the moon is shining; show me the glint of light on broken glass.

— Anton Chekhov
author of *The Cherry Orchard*

DAY 54

"Don't tell, show." You've heard this before.

What does it mean? It means, don't tell us about anger, show us how the person is acting. If you do it well, we'll feel the anger.

Don't tell the readers what to feel. Show them the characters and the situation, and that feeling of anger — or sorrow or love or honesty or justice — will waken in them. "Thinking" and "believing" are abstract. Show instead the physical actions and concrete details of what your characters are doing. This will let your readers do the thinking and knowing — and believing.

Today I wrote _____ *words.* _____

Do you think you have been able to achieve believability in your novel
by showing, not telling?

Give an example.

DAY 55

Those of us who had a perfectly happy childhood should be able to sue for deprivation of literary royalties.

— Chris Patten
author of *The Tory Case*

It's okay to have trouble with writing, with keeping at it, with making your prose perfect.

This is what Jacques Barzun, who taught at Columbia University, suggested to his students:

> Convince yourself that you are working in clay, not marble, on paper, not eternal bronze: Let that first sentence be as stupid as it wishes. . . . Just put it down; and then another. Your whole first paragraph or first page may have to be guillotined after your piece is finished; but there can be no second paragraph until you have a first.

The only thing you need be concerned about now is that you finish a first draft of your novel. And keep reminding yourself that's what it is: a first draft.

Today I wrote _____ *words.*

How close are you to being finished with your first draft — 85 percent?
90 percent? 95 percent?

56
DAY

Your audience is one single reader. I have found that sometimes it helps to pick out one person — a real person you know, or an imagined person, and write to that one.

— John Steinbeck
author of *The Grapes of Wrath*

A typical working manuscript doesn't look finished. It consists of piles of pages. Each pile is a chapter, plus perhaps a file folder overflowing with notes and journals.

Think of your working manuscript as a growing child. It is a book that eventually will be finished, just as a child will eventually become an adult. Think of yourself as a firm parent to the child of your creative mind, so that you will be proud of the manuscript when you finally send it out into the world.

Today I wrote _____ *words.*

In terms of years, how old is your novel at this stage of development?

_____

_____

_____

_____

_____

_____

_____

DAY 57

All writers are vain, selfish and lazy, and at the very bottom of their motives lies a mystery. Writing a book is a long, exhausting struggle, like a long bout of some painful illness. One would never undertake such a thing if one were not driven by some demon whom one can neither resist nor understand.

— George Orwell
author of *1984*

By now you should have written close to 240 pages or 60,000 words.

But are these pages a novel?

Ask yourself: Have I told a story with a beginning, a middle and an end? Have I raised a question and answered it? Have I presented a puzzle and then solved it?

You will be able to remedy any of these problems when you are editing. During the editing process you will not only be deleting and re-writing, but also writing new material, and you can expect your novel to grow in length as well as in quality.

Today I wrote _____ *words.*

Make some notes about any problems you think your novel has. Once
you are editing, use this list to remind yourself of what you need to do.

Do a spelling and grammar check.

This won't get rid of all of your mistakes, but it will provide you with a clean draft that is ready for the editing that you will soon begin to do.

Today I wrote _____ *words.*

Were you amazed at how many errors you turned up?

_____

_____

Make a list of the words you commonly misspelled.

_____

_____

_____

_____

_____

I love being a writer. What I can't stand is all the paper-
work.

— Peter DeVries
author of *The Tunnel of Love*

Print out a hard copy of your book.

You are about to start the most important
part of the writing process — rewriting. And
you want to do it with fresh paper and a fresh
start.

Today I wrote _____ *words.*

Does the working title you wrote down on Day 7 still seem right for
your book? If not, what might be better?

_____

_____

_____

_____

And that last line you wrote on Day 10 — does it work? Does it bring
your story to a satisfying close?

_____

_____

_____

_____

60 DAY

Sleep on your writing; take a walk over it; scrutinize it in the morning; review it in the afternoon; digest it after a meal; let it sleep in your drawer a twelvemonth; never venture a whisper about it to your friend, if he be an author especially.

— A. Bronson Alcott
author of *Concord Days*

Congratulations.

You have achieved a lot. You have written a first draft.

Take the day off. Don't read a book. Don't write a letter. Go to a movie. Climb a mountain. Ride a bike. Enjoy the world beyond your home and desk.

The First Edit

61 DAY

What is writing a novel like?

1. The beginning: A ride through a spring wood.
2. The middle: The Gobi Desert.
3. The end: A night with a lover . . ..

— Edith Wharton
author of *The House of Mirth*

Sit with the hard copy of your manuscript and read it — out loud if at all possible. All of it.

Read it as if you were a general reader, not the book's author. You need to step back and look at the story as objectively as you can — as if it was written by someone you do not know.

Pause only to jot notes about changes that need to be made.

Watch for problems with organization such as continuity, logical time sequence, suspense building, missing details, and characters that need further development. Also note awkward sentences and words that are used incorrectly.

When you read a section that is a fine piece of writing — a well-balanced sentence, a great description, a fresh metaphor — stop and recognize how you feel. Remember this moment.

Today I edited _____ *pages.*

Write down a few sentences that you think are particularly fine.

62 DAY

When you finish reading a chapter, ask yourself: What is the purpose of this chapter? What needs to be cut from it? What is missing that needs to be added? What is said in this chapter that would make the reader want to continue reading to find out what happens next?

Then begin to edit:

- Rewriting (again and again).
- Reorganizing.

Today I edited _____ *pages.*

What is the name or number of the chapter that you think works best
in your novel? Figure out that chapter's distinguishing features, then
see if the other chapters share them.

DAY 63

> Good novels are not written, they are rewritten. Great novels are diamonds mined from layered rewrites.
>
> — Andrew Jute
> in *Writing a Thriller*

There are three types of manuscript:

1. The *working manuscript* is rough, like an unfinished sculpture. It resembles the final work, but it has jagged edges and lacks polish. The working manuscript is the book you just wrote.

2. The *self-edited manuscript* is produced by the writer when he or she moves from the role of writer to the role of editor. You are not only the first reader of your book, you are also the first editor.

3. The *final manuscript* is smooth and polished, and the best that you can do. It is ready to go to the printer — in your opinion. (Your next editor may think otherwise.)

During the next 26 days you will be working on your "self-edited manuscript." You have just completed your first read-through; today you will begin to rewrite, to delete, and to add new material. Then you will do these steps all over again. In addition to your editing I will give you assignments each day that will help you clean up your manuscript.

Now to the editing

Around 14 B.C., the Roman poet Horace observed that writers should attempt "to say at once what ought at once to be said." In other words, grab your reader by the throat from your very first sentence. If Roman poets had to get right to the point, so do you.

Begin your editing by re-reading your first page. Does it "say at once what ought at once to be said"? If you hadn't written it, would the first page be powerful enough to persuade you to read the rest of the book?

Today I edited _____ *pages.* _____

Does your first page need a grabber? _____

_____

_____

_____

_____

_____

_____

_____

64

No author dislikes to be edited as much as he dislikes not to be published.

— Russell Lynes
author of *Highbrow, Lowbrow, Middlebrow*

The great science fiction writer Ray Bradbury once said, "Any man who keeps working is not a failure. He may not be a great writer, but if he applies the old-fashioned virtues of hard, constant labor, he'll eventually make some kind of career for himself as a writer."

Now you are going to make that career for yourself by editing and polishing and fixing this novel of yours. Yes, turning first draft sentences into polished prose is hard work.

Today I edited _____ *pages.* _____

In one sentence, say what you learned about writing from your first
day of editing.

_____

_____

_____

Now write it on an index card and keep it somewhere that you'll see
and remember it.

_____

_____

_____

65

DAY

It is perfectly okay to write garbage — as long as you edit brilliantly.

— C. J. Cherryh
author of *Cyteen*

Choose a short scene that you have written, make a copy of it, and put the copy away. Now edit that scene.

After you finish editing the entire book, revisit the selected scene in its edited form and make a copy of it as well.

Finally, show the two versions of the scene — without telling which is which — to a smart reader, and ask him or her which is better written, more interesting. Maybe now you are half finished and it still could be better.

Today I edited _____ *pages.*

Briefly describe the scene you will choose for this comparison.

_____

_____

_____

_____

_____

_____

_____

_____

66 DAY

Here is novelist and memoirist Mary-Ann Tirone Smith explaining how she edits her first drafts. This will give you an idea of what a writer needs to do before a manuscript is "finished."

I write the first draft of each of my novels in longhand in a spiral notebook.

Then I sit in a cozy chair, under a lovely lamp, pen in hand, and I read what I've got, scribbling in the margins as I go. If I can't fit a change or revision in the margin, I rip a page out of the back of the notebook, assign it a letter and stick it behind the page where it will go. Then I type it all.

Then, back to the chair with the great lamp, and I do the same thing again — write all over it and stick in any long revisions. Then I type it again.

Then I give the manuscript to four writer friends — one at a time. When friend A returns it with comments, I do another revision and then pass it on to friend B, etc. Let's see, that's nine drafts. Then I give it to my long-suffering husband who is, to my great fortune, a language teacher, and he cleans it up.

I read and revise once more before sending it on to my agent who will ask for minor changes or big changes. Then there are usually two revisions with an editor and then one with the line editor. Then the publisher mails me the page proofs and I get my last shot at final revisions.

Today I edited _____ *pages.* _____

On average how many times have you re-written a page? _____

_____

_____

_____

_____

_____

_____

_____

_____

DAY 67

pr: How much rewriting do you do?

eh: It depends. I rewrote the ending of *Farewell to Arms*, the last page of it, 39 times before I was satisfied.

pr: Was there some technical problem there? What was it that had stumped you?

eh: Getting the words right.

— Ernest Hemingway
The Paris Review interview 1956: "The Art of Fiction"

The novelist Bernard Malamud, who wrote *The Natural*, said this about the stages of a manuscript:

> First drafts are for learning what your [book] is about. Revision is working with that knowledge to enlarge and enhance an idea, to reform it . . . . Revision is one of the true pleasures of writing.

Revision is the "growing up" process that a book must go through to achieve its maximum potential. It involves hard work and it may be frustrating at times. Yet a writer who does not revise almost certainly dooms his or her work to an early death. Revision can be the difference between a salable book and one that lies forgotten.

Many writers think that the first draft of their manuscripts need only a few minor changes before being sent out. Change a word or two, fix the typos, and editors will beg to publish the book. Not true.

You must be unsentimental enough to face the fact that your working manuscript is not perfect. Then you must be tough enough to revise it without mercy. You must be willing to take out material that you spent months on, if that's what you decide is needed. You must also have the patience to improve individual paragraphs and sentences. Weakness at this level will translate into weaknesses in the overall book. When you see something that isn't right, you must fix it. If you can fix it, start fixing it. If you can't fix it, kill it. Self-editing will be a waste of time if you are not demanding of yourself.

Today I edited _____ *pages.*

Write down several examples of how you have "fixed" a sentence.

What is important is the story. Because when we are all dust and teeth and kicked-up bits of skin — when we're dancing with our own skeletons — our words might be all that's left of us.

— Alexandra Fuller
author of *Scribbling the Cat*

Incorporate into your manuscript the necessary changes and corrections that you recorded during your read-through yesterday. This may require cutting, rewriting, or writing new material.

Today I edited   *pages.*

Rate from 1 to 10 where you stand in terms of being finished with your
self-edit.

DAY 69

Books aren't written — they're rewritten. Including your own. It is one of the hardest things to accept, especially after the seventh rewrite hasn't quite done it.

— Michael Crichton
author of *The Andromeda Strain*

Bad writers do not rewrite. Good writers re-write. Superb writers keep rewriting again and again. It is as simple as that.

All of us write too many words. The best gift we can give our readers is less of what we write.

Keep in mind that you need to be clear about your purpose here, then take out the clutter.

- Cut all clichés, jargon, and phrases that weigh down sentences ("cool as a cucumber," "pretty as a picture," etc.).
- Cast out current buzz words such as "belief system," "networking," "coming from," "support system."
- Watch out for repetitions. While there's a place for deliberate repetition, most of us are guilty of lazy repetition, using the same word repeatedly on a page or even in a single paragraph or sentence.

Today I edited _____ *pages.*

What are some of the clichés and gobbledygook that you edited out
of your novel?

My books aren't trying to fathom the mysteries of human existence. I'm an entertainer.

— Bernard Cornwall
author of *Death of Kings*

Every word in a sentence should work for you. Get rid of phrases that do nothing but weigh the sentence down. For example, never say "exact opposite," say "opposite"; never say "owing to the fact that," say "because."

Watch out for unconsciously funny phrases, such as: "I had a gut feeling about his lunch plans" or "They're cutting my throat behind my back."

The problem here is that you're trafficking in metaphors that have become so clichéd you don't even think about the literal meaning. If you did, you'd never say "cut my throat behind my back." Keep your metaphors fresh and vivid and this won't happen.

Today I edited _____ *pages.* _____

What are some of the meaningless phrases that you cut from your novel?

_____

_____

_____

_____

What are some of the words you have replaced? And with what?

_____

_____

_____

_____

_____

**DAY 71**

Let me . . . tell you why I prefer writing to real life: You can rewrite. A novel, for example, can be cleaned up, altered, trimmed, improved. Life, on the other hand, is one big messy rough draft.

— Harlan Coben
author of *Six Years*

While rewriting you focus closely on words and sentences. But to reorganize you need to step back and look at your work as a whole. You may discover organizational and/or logical problems that need to be dealt with.

Perhaps you will cut some more, and perhaps you will add. Do whatever is necessary to remedy the organizational issues you have found.

During the writing process did you create some scenes for which you had no place at the time? Might you have an ideal spot for one or two of them now?

Sometimes reorganization is major. Once you finish a draft, you may decide to flip the structure, to start with what is now the ending. Or you may break open the book and grab a scene or section from the middle and move it up front. It doesn't matter. What does matter is that the story have a beginning, middle, and end.

Go back to your original outline, even your original notes, and check to see whether you skipped any major or minor points. Should you tear apart the manuscript and add a missing piece? Or should you leave it alone?

Today I edited _____ *pages.*

What surprised you the most about reorganizing your novel?

There is no way of writing well and also of writing easily.

— Anthony Trollope
author of *The Way We Live Now*

Cut unnecessary chunks from the manuscript so that the story can move faster.

You must even be willing to remove favorite passages that especially please you if they are not important to the story. As William Faulkner said, "In writing, you must kill your darlings."

Today I edited _____ *pages.*

Write down some of your "darlings" that need to be killed — perhaps you can use them in your next book.

_____

_____

_____

_____

_____

_____

_____

_____

73

Cutting is a beginning. But replacing place-holder words with better ones is another editing task. Be specific, not general — "knife and fork," not "eating utensils"; "a black '67 Cadillac," not "a car." Stephen King is very good at this kind of specificity.

Today I edited _____ *pages.* _____

List some concrete words you've put in and the abstract words you
took out.

Metaphors have a way of holding the most truth in the least space.

— Orson Scott Card
author of *How to Write Science Fiction and Fantasy*

Every reader hates excessive metaphors. Sometimes, however, a writer can use excessive metaphors for humor. For example, H. L. Menchen once described President Harding's speaking style this way, "It reminds me of a string of wet sponges; it reminds me of tattered washing on the line; it reminds me of stale bean-soup, of college yells, of dogs barking idiotically through endless nights."

Don't put yourself in Harding's shoes.

Go back and cut one metaphor or simile from each page. Hint: To quickly locate your metaphors and similes, do a computer search for "as" and "like" in each chapter.

Today I edited _____ *pages.* _____

List some of the metaphors and similes that you cut from your book.

_____

_____

_____

_____

_____

_____

_____

_____

DAY 75

I don't mean to sell the poet so long or at such great length, but I do this principally because the world doesn't esteem the poet very much. They don't understand where we are coming from. They don't understand the use for us. They don't understand if there is any use. We are the masters of the superior secret, not they. Not they. Remember that when you write.

— James Dickey
author of *Deliverance*

Remember, you don't need to have written a book to get into heaven. But if you do write one, that book will always be yours, up there on the shelf, and proving to you — and everyone else — that you see the world as larger than one life, and that you have the imagination and the creative juices to create something out of nothing. That, my friend, is no small achievement.

Today I edited _____ *pages.*

Write a few sentences expressing how you feel about your book.

DAY **76**

The road to hell is paved with adverbs.

— Stephen King
author of *Carrie*

Start on page one and delete one adjective
or adverb from every paragraph in the book.

Today I edited _____ *pages.* _____

Read five pages of a Stephen King novel and see if there are any adverbs
you would cut.

DAY 77

In the case of hunting, it's important to maintain silence; in the case of writing, to maintain an incessant clacking of keystrokes. Ultimately, I found that success for each often came down to my ability to endure discomfort and boredom long enough for the desired result to happen along, magically, on its own.

— Steven Rinella
author of *Meat Eater*

Get rid of unnecessary punctuation marks: exclamation marks, excessive commas, single quotation marks, parentheses and italics. Again, read from the first page to the last.

Elmore Leonard listed cutting exclamation marks as one of his ten rules for writing a book — "You are allowed no more than two or three per 100,000 words of prose."

Hint: Find those exclamation marks by doing a computer search.

Today I edited _____ *pages.* _____

How many unnecessary punctuation marks did you cut today?

78 DAY

The only thing I was fit for was to be a writer, and this notion rested solely on my suspicion that I would never be fit for real work, and that writing didn't require any.

— Russell Baker
author of *Growing Up*

Get rid of any foreign words or phrases you don't absolutely need. Get rid of unnecessary fancy words, vulgar language or images, and graphic scenes of sex.

The hardest scenes to write are good sex scenes. The less said, and the more implied, the better.

Today I edited _____ *pages.*

What was the best sex scene you ever read? Why was it so effective?

_____

_____

_____

_____

_____

_____

_____

_____

Look at the final page of each chapter in your novel, and consider whether you can shorten it. As I mentioned, the best time to end a chapter is with a sentence that will catapult the reader into the next chapter. See if you can close out each of your chapters a little bit sooner and in a way that will raise a question, hint at something new to be discovered or promise more adventure.

In the novel I am working on now, I used these last lines for three of the chapters:

CHAPTER 3
I did not turn around. I knew she was watching me.

CHAPTER 13
She moved through the jet bridge, know-ing he was in step behind her. In the morning, she would wake in Madrid seven thousand miles away from her unhappy marriage; having spent the night snuggled up beside a man who was not her husband.

CHAPTER 20
"I'm two weeks overdue with my period."

Today I edited _____ *pages.*

Does each chapter end with enough drama to keep the reader reading? Record a "yes" or "no" for each chapter.

DAY 80

Put your heart into what you are writing. If you can't laugh at your own characters, or shed a tear for them, or even get angry at one of them, no one else will either.

— Johanna Lindsey
author of *When Passion Rules*

Now that you have written and edited (and re-edited) the first draft of your novel, there is one more task to accomplish before you finish your book. You need to look at each chapter as a whole, as a story unto itself. You need each of your chapters to have a beginning, a middle and an end.

Individual chapters, of course, are linked to what has come before and what will happen next. An individual chapter makes a contribution to the whole story, but needs to tell its own story. Doing this is not as difficult as it seems; it just takes a little work.

Ask yourself the following questions about your first chapter:

- What is the purpose of the chapter?
- What is the central information the chapter is carrying forward?
- What is the secret or surprise in this chapter?

- Have you removed any dialogue or details that don't contribute to either the plot or the development of your characters?
- Does the chapter have a beginning, a middle, an end?
- Does the last line of the chapter intrigue the reader to keep reading?

Having answered these questions for chapter one, move on and do the same for each subsequent chapter.

Today I edited _____ *pages.*

Once you've asked these questions about every chapter,
comment on what you learned about shaping a chapter.

DAY 81

Read your novel into a digital recorder, and then play it back while keeping a copy of the written text handy. Listen for scenes that don't work, language that draws too much attention to itself, and make notes on the hard copy. Later on, make cuts to solve whatever problems you jotted down. Cut and cut and cut toward the core of the novel, the essence of what your story is about.

Today I edited _____ *pages.* _____

Pick a scene about which you're undecided. Write down the ways in
which it works and the ways in which it doesn't. If you're still undecided,
cut the scene.

DAY 82

I have been successful probably because I have always realized that I knew nothing about writing and have merely tried to tell an interesting story entertainingly.

— Edgar Rice Burroughs
author of *Tarzan of the Apes*

Norman Mailer always made the point that good writers spend more time working on the beginning and the ending of their books than on what comes in between.

Think of the opening as something special that will snag the reader and make him or her keep reading.

Today I edited _____ *pages.* _____

Now that you know how your novel ends, reread how it begins. Now
that you know what will follow, how can you improve the opening to
make sure that the reader is hooked?

**83**

The human race needs the novel. We need all the experience we can get. Those who say the novel is dead can't write them.

— Bernard Malamud
author of *A New Life*

Choose a half dozen great novels and read only the first sentences of each. Type them out and then type out your first sentence. How do you compare with some of the best writers in the world? Look at their opening lines and think about how to rewrite yours.

Today I edited _____ *pages.* _____

Write down the first sentences from a few novels that you admire. What
do they have in common?

_____

_____

_____

_____

_____

_____

_____

**DAY 84**

If I ask you to think about something, you can decide not to. But if I make you feel something? Now I have your attention.

— Lisa Cron
author of *Wired for Story:*
The Writer's Guide to Using Brain Science
to Hook Readers from the Very First Sentence

Read further into the first pages of your book. You may discover a better starting point for your book tucked into a paragraph that comes later in the telling. Sometimes we have the habit of warming up before we say or write something worthy. See if you have done that with the opening of your novel.

Rewrite your first scene. Having finished a first draft, you find that you understand much better what your book needs in the first chapter, and what can be cut. You will also see that you are a much better writer than you were when you started.

Today I edited _____ *pages.* _____

Count the words in the first scene in both your first draft and second
draft. The scene should be shorter in the second draft. If not, work on
it some more.

DAY 85

The end of a novel, like the end of a children's dinner-party, must be made up of sweetmeats and sugar-plums.

— Anthony Trollope
author of *Barchester Towers*

Rewrite the climactic scene that resolves the conflict and ends your novel. You want to craft the ending so that it satisfies the reader, rewarding him or her for taking the journey with you. The reader should come away from the book thinking that the time was well spent. You may have created the new *Harry Potter* series or written the next *The Corrections*. Either way, the reader will thank you for telling them a great tale.

Today I edited _____ *pages.* _____

Is your ending memorable? Why or why not? Is it memorable for its
events, for its language, or both?

_____

_____

_____

_____

_____

_____

_____

_____

86 DAY

Being a novelist, I consider myself superior to the saint, the scientist, the philosopher, and the poet, who are all great masters of different bits of man alive, but never the whole hog.

— D. H. Lawrence
in *Why the Novel Matters*

Review your manuscript and make sure you have given your readers a picture of your characters early in the story. Readers don't need to know everything, but they do need to know what is physically important about each character. Use the five senses to bring your characters alive on paper.

Today I edited _____ *pages.* _____

How many senses did you use to describe your protagonist? _____

_____

_____

_____

_____

_____

_____

_____

I don't know much about creative writing programs. But they're not telling the truth if they don't teach: one, that writing is hard work, and, two, that you have to give up a great deal of life, your personal life, to be a writer.

— Doris Lessing
author of *The Golden Notebook*

The short story writer Raymond Carver said he knew a story was finished when he found himself going through it once and putting commas in, then going through it again and taking the commas out. Is that how you feel?

Well, you're done now.

That is, after you have completed the assignment on the next page.

Today I edited _____ *pages.*

Do a spelling and grammar check again. You'd be surprised at the number of errors one makes while editing.

Perform a "Find" for all double spaces between words and "Replace" them with single spaces.

DAY 88

Well into adulthood writing has never gotten easier. It still only ever begins badly, and there are no guarantees that this is not the day when the jig is finally up. And yet, I don't for a moment forget that this is not a life of mining coal, waiting tables or answering someone's phone for a living.

— David Rakoff
author of *Half Empty*

A book takes a long time to write, and as you write you get better, and the more you write, the better you get. It is as simple as that.

As you reread your first draft, you saw that you went well beyond your original notes and ideas. And with each step of editing you have improved your manuscript further by applying the rewriting and reorganizing techniques you have learned.

You have been working for 88 days. You are not finished — this is only the first draft, but you have made tremendous progress.

Once your book *is* finished you will realize that you are a better writer than when you started, with more discipline and better writing habits. So much so that you'll want to start from scratch and write your book again. But don't do that. It is now time to prepare to sell your novel.

Today I edited _____ *pages.* _____

Think about it. Do you feel that you are a better writer now than when
you started to write this novel? In what ways?

_____

_____

_____

_____

_____

_____

_____

Preparing to Sell Your Novel

Write out of love; write out of instinct; write out of reason.
But always for money.

— Louis Untermeyer
author of *Moses*

To begin the process of finding a publisher, write a one-sentence selling line about your novel. Make this one sentence so intriguing that it catches everyone's attention. It must go to the core of the book. It is your "selling hook." For example, "My novel is the Jewish version of *The Da Vinci Code*."

Write a 200-word "selling line" for your book. Then cut it to 100 words.
Then 40. See if you can cut it to 10.

No writer should ever publish a book until he has first read it to a woman.

— Van Wyck Brooks
in *The Writer in America*

Write a short description of your novel. It should be a paragraph or two that can appear on the back cover, and will persuade someone who is browsing to buy your book over another. Often at a publishing house some young assistant is assigned to write this "selling blurb," but you can do a better job because you know your book, and an assistant may just skim the text to understand the plot.

This is what I wrote to sell my book *The Caddie Who Played with Hickory*:

Before there were titanium woods and graphite shafts, golf clubs were made from the wood of hickory trees and had intriguing names like cleek, mashie, and jigger. Golf was a game played not with high-tech equipment, but with skill, finesse, and creativity. And the greatest hickory player of all time was Walter Hagen — until the day he met a teenage caddie at a country club outside Chicago.

With this paragraph I set the stage for the expectations of my readers, who I knew would be mostly golfers. I also knew that today's golfers might not be that familiar with the history of the game. In addition, I wanted the reader to know that the climactic match would be between Walter Hagen and the protagonist of the story, the caddie.

Your "selling blurb" should fit on this page.

 **DAY 91**

If you don't write for publication, there is little point in writing at all.

— Gabriel Garcia Marquez
author of *One Hundred Years of Solitude*

Write a short statement about yourself.

Now you are selling you. This statement will be included when you send your manuscript to agents or editors. You need to impress whoever reads your statement with your personality, your wit and your knowledge of the subject of your novel. You need to brag while at the same time tell the truth, and the best way to do that is to be clever and modest.

Sound professional. Don't write: "I always wanted to be a writer . . . ." or "I can write better than the junk I see . . . ." or "My friends have read my novel and they think it is great."

The following is what F. Scott Fitzgerald might have written about himself:

I once said, "The rich are different," to which my friend Ernest Hemingway replied, "Yes, they have more money." Ernie was wrong about that, as he was wrong about many things, including his talent and mine. It is more than money that separates classes. It is the self-assurance of place.

All writers are shaped by where they come from. I grew up Catholic and Irish in genteel St. Paul, Minnesota, where my family lived in a different social world than did our neighbors. We were close enough to see the "right families of St. Paul, but not close enough to be one of them.

While I was lucky enough to attend good schools, i.e., the Newman School and Princeton, I was never part of our wealthy neighbors' society. That world, therefore, has fascinated me, as do the money and the power that insulate that world.

In my first two novels I wrote about what money does to people, and in my new novel, *The Great Gatsby*, I return to the topic to tell the story of this world of wealth and power and the fate of someone who attempts to make himself a place at that table.

Your statement about yourself should fit here.

DAY 92

Most people won't realize that writing is a craft. You have to take your apprenticeship in it like anything else.

— Katherine Ann Porter
author of *Ship of Fools*

Whether you are submitting your manuscript electronically or on paper, it needs to be properly formatted.

The following are basic requirements, but some agents, editors and publishers have their own particular guidelines and you should research how your book should be submitted. If there are no specifications designated by an agent, you should follow these instructions carefully.

Page formatting:

- The font: 12-point, serif.
- Line spacing: double-spaced.
- Margins: one inch on all four sides.
- Page numbers should be consecutive from the title page to the last page of text.
- New chapters should start halfway down a new page.
- Make no mention of rights or copyright.

(Doing so labels you as an amateur.)

Printing your manuscript:

- Paper: 8½" x 11", standard 20-pound bond (not high-gloss), white. Do not use three-hole-punch paper.
- Printer: laser or ink-jet.
- Binding: should not be bound in any way.

Carefully scroll through your entire formatted manuscript to check that
the layout is consistent throughout.

 **DAY 93**

I had thought . . . the hardest part of publishing a book would be selling the idea, and then writing the book, but I was wrong. The hardest part was trying to get people to buy it.

— Louisa Thomas
author of *Conscience: Two Soldiers, Two Pacifists, One Family — A Test of Will and Faith in World War I*

Because some literary agents are only interested in receiving a portion of a manuscript for initial review, you should create a new file on your computer that contains only the first 50 pages or so of your novel. Cut the story off at a point where the reader will want to know what happens next.

Print a copy of your full manuscript and a copy of the 50-page sample. Examine both carefully to make sure that there are no problems with their appearance.

DAY 94

Of course no writers ever forget their first acceptance. One fine day when I was seventeen I had my first, second and third, all in the same morning's mail. Oh, I'm here to tell you, dizzy with excitement is no mere phrase!

— Truman Capote
author of *In Cold Blood*

It is now time to find a literary agent to represent your novel and show it to appropriate publishers if you are not going to self-publish.

In seeking an agent, remember that you are an unknown and the top agents are always overwhelmed with clients and would-be clients. Aim for agents just beginning their careers. Agents often specialize in specific genres of books, so make the agents you approach all represent the genre of the novel you have written.

Your agent will not be your best friend. He or she will guide you in the process of getting your novel published. An agent may even help you with the content. If you find an agent who says something like, "You have talent, but your writing needs work," then sign up. He or she may help to revise your book before an editor even sees it.

To begin your search for a literary agent:

- Check out "Resources on the Internet for Writers" at the end of this book.

- On the Internet, search on such key words as "agent" and "author representation."
- Check the acknowledgement pages of books similar to yours for the names of the authors' agents.
- Do not pay any agent a "reader's fee" or use an agent who requests a reader's fee before deciding whether to represent you.

If you are self-publishing your book you do not need an agent to represent you. You can manage all the phases of the publishing process yourself and not share the profits of your book with anyone.

List the of names of some literary agents who specialize in books like
yours. Include their contact information.

DAY 95

Your agent relationship is akin to a marriage. Emotions, finances, and trust are all tangled up and can be easily wounded if you aren't careful. Similarly, that agent can be one of your most loyal and cherished people on earth. Your literary spouse of sorts.

— Sarah McCoy
author of *The Baker's Daughter*

Write a very brief cover letter to each agent. You might begin:

> I recently read and very much admired _____, and saw that you are _____'s agent.

> *or:*

> My friend/acquaintance _____, who is represented by you, suggested you as a possible agent for my book.

> *or:*

> I read your article in _____ about the book business, and was hoping that you might consider my novel.

> *or:*

> I attended your lecture at _____.

If the agent accepts email submissions (and most do), you should include in your letter the one-paragraph description of your novel that indicates the genre, and the brief paragraph about yourself.

Are you considering sending your manuscript to more than one agent at the same time? If so, you should be aware that most agents are offended by multiple submissions. They want to be told up front if you're doing this, because reading a manuscript that's been submitted to other agents at the same time means they may be wasting their time.

If an agent wants to receive a hard copy submission, then your mailing should contain:

- Your cover letter to the agent that includes the one-paragraph description of your novel indicating the genre, and the brief paragraph about yourself.
- The 50-page sample of your novel.
- A size #10, stamped, self-addressed envelope (SASE) for the agent to send a response. (Your 50 pages will not be returned.)

Create a list of agents who would be appropriate for you book. If you are submitting to more than one at a time, choose five. Otherwise, choose one. Then send out your 25–50 page sample with your query letter. Do it today.

Having an agent who will be honest with you is wonderful. Having an agent you can be honest with is even better.

— Lydia Netzer
author of *Shine, Shine, Shine*

During my career I have had six agents, each working at a different agency. Agents are not (usually) would-be writers or failed writers. They are business people who are looking for good, interesting, profitable books. They need to make money to stay in business, and if you can make them money with your book they will represent you whether they like you personally or not. Or whether you like them or not.

Some agents have been around for a long time. They have seen it all and dealt with all kinds of writers who have walked through their doors. You won't surprise them.

Some agents are warm and inspiring and try to keep their clients' spirits up. If you find such an agent, that's a bonus, but don't expect it. This is a business relationship, not a friendship. Don't pester an agent with phone calls, or expect him or her to talk you through a down period. Your family and friends can help you with that, I hope. Don't use up your agent's patience and good will on emotional issues; rely on him or her for professional advice and good salesmanship. That is your agent's job: to sell your book for the best possible price.

Finally, don't sign with any agent who wants you to pay money up front. You don't pay agents to represent you; they get paid by taking a percentage of your advance and royalties.

Write down all the qualities you seek in an agent.

Now cross out everything but "experienced," "smart," "aggressive" and
"civilized to deal with."

97

Are you thinking about self-publishing your novel?

On his website, Underdown.org, Harold Underdown has this sage advice in an article titled "Self-Publish or Not?":

My advice is that you do not consider self-publishing until you have spent at least a few years working on your writing, making submissions, and learning about the business of publishing. That won't be wasted time, because even if you don't get published, if you do decide to self-publish later you will be much better equipped to do so successfully. You will have a more polished manuscript or manuscripts. You will also have learned something about what you need to do which is, very briefly, get your book edited, illustrated, designed, promoted, reviewed, and distributed — things a publisher routinely does, but which are difficult and expensive for an individual to do.

To read more about self-publishing see "Self-Publishing Your Novel" and "Resources on the Internet for Writers" at the end of this book.

If you decide to self-publish, list the ways you would promote and market your novel. (Actually, this is useful even if you go with a publisher — an author needs to do everything possible to market his or her work, and even a well-known publishing house will count on you to do a lot of the work.)

Publishers don't nurse you; they buy and sell you.

— P.D. James
author of *Death Comes to Pemberley*

DAY 98

Regardless of whether you go with a publisher or self-publish your novel you want to release an e-book version as well as a print version. Over the past few years more e-books have been sold than print copies. Your goal is to have as many people as possible read what you have written, and e-books present you with a much wider audience.

Do a search on the Internet for "e-book vs print" to read extended
discussions of the pros and cons of each form of publication.

DAY 99

Coleridge was a drug addict. Poe was an alcoholic. Marlowe was killed by a man whom he was treacherously trying to stab. Pope took money to keep a woman's name out of a satire then wrote a piece so that she could still be recognized anyhow. Chatterton killed himself. Byron was accused of incest. Do you still want to be a writer — and if so, why?

— Bennett Cerf
co-founder of Random House

You now want to get out and meet other writers. Find out if your local community college or YMCA or library has a writing group where you can meet other writers.

Check out the Association of Writers & Writing Programs at www.AWPwriter.org, and become a member. Through the AWP you can get lists of centers, networks, workshops, foundations, seminars and summer conferences for writers that you can attend.

It is mind-boggling, the number of opportunities that are available to meet other writers to share what you have written, to learn what real readers think of your prose and to exchange ideas on getting an agent and marketing your book.

You've written your novel. Do you still want to be a writer — and if so, why?

100 **DAY O**

Congratulations. You've done it.

You kept at it and you wrote your novel. Yes, you will have more editing to do (there is always more editing to do), but you overcame all of the distractions in your life to finish your book. That is a huge accomplishment and you should be proud. Not everyone can write a novel. In fact, very few people have the discipline, direction and dedication to complete a book. You did. You have created something from nothing. With your imagination, creative impulse and perseverance you have given us a new window into the world through your imagination and knowledge. That's an achievement that should make you proud.

Now: Take everything you've learned and start writing your next novel.

Resources

Self-Publishing Your Novel

The age of the "gatekeepers" — the large trade publishing houses — is over. Anyone can publish anything they want and no one can stop them.

Traditionally we have had four types of book publishers:

- Trade publishers, who sell to the general public
- Small presses
- Academic presses
- Vanity presses, which authors pay to publish their books

With the perfecting of desk-top publishing combined with access to the Internet, we are seeing the rise of a fifth type, the self publisher. Today, writers can make their own decision on what to publish and when; they can also retain larger royalties than they would receive from traditional publishers.

Being your own publisher

If you decide to publish your own book you must function as its publisher. You have to fill all the following roles or hire people to fill them:

- Writer
- Line Editor
- Copy editor
- Book designer
- Cover designer
- Publicist
- Sales person
- Website designer
- Social Media Expert

To purchase most of these services in one place, you can work with a company that specializes in helping you self publish. These companies are in business to profit from writers who think they have a book others will want to read. They make their money by not only printing books and facilitating distribution, but also by providing — at a total cost of $1,000 to $10,000 — such services as editing, design and promotion.

Spend your money wisely. If not, self publishing your novel could cost you as much as

$10,000, and most likely you will never earn back that amount from book sales.

Hire out some tasks

If you decide not to use the edit, design and sales services of your self-publishing company, you must then hire independent professionals to do these tasks.

Editing. You will need an editor — or two. Editing is not a task for friends or relatives, unless they are professionals in the field.

You are looking for two types of editors.

A *Line Editor* will look at sentence and paragraph structure, the way you develop a scene, and what works dramatically on the page.

A *Copy Editor* will make sure that your prose is consistent, there are no misspelled words, and the grammar and punctuation are correct. Think of this person as a traffic cop, and you're a little kid at a school crossing. Listen to what the Copy Editor has to say.

Editors you hire could be people who work as editors at the local newspaper, at magazines, or even at book companies. Often full-time editors take on freelance work.

You can also check on Craigs List or the Jobs Wanted section in the newspaper classified ads to see if any editors are seeking clients. Some editors work part-time from home. Try to find someone local; it is best to meet face to face at least once if possible. And don't forget to ask for — and check — references.

Kirkus Magazine has an editing service, and other publications such as Poets & Writers and The Writer's Chronicle list editing services.

Design. Once your manuscript is thoroughly edited you will have to hire a *Book Designer*. Do not try to convince yourself that because you can write a book you can also design it. I have found from experience that most "word" people are not "design" people. It is a different skill, a talent that comes from the other side of the brain. Nothing turns off a reader as fast as a book that looks (and is) unreadable. If you want someone to read your novel, it must be visually inviting.

Then you will need an *Illustrator* to design your cover.

Promotion. Your *Publicist* will open some doors for you by arranging to have reviews published both locally and on the Internet, and by setting up interviews and maybe even appearances on local TV.

To promote the book, you will also need a website, a Facebook page and a Twitter account. That means hiring a *Web Designer* and possibly a *Social Media Expert*.

Your other job — marketing

Will anyone besides your mother know about and want to read what you have self-published? To become a successful novelist you must also become a successful self-promoter.

Seek a niche. You have to seek out the marketing niche where your novel might have a built-in audience. If you find your niche audience you will sell more copies of your novel.

For example, when I recently wrote three golf novels, I researched and contacted golf bloggers and publications. I also contacted, through golf associations, golf shops around the country. I sent emails to every golf-related organization or individual I could find on the Internet. I sent them an email with a package of information: an image of the jacket, a brief bio, a summary of the plot, and quotes about my books from other golf writers and players.

Buy a review. It is possible to pay for reviews. Kirkus as well as Publishers Weekly now have review services for self-published writers. Kirkus charges from $425 to $575, and Publishers Weekly has a variety of offerings beginning at $150.

Find a hook. If your novel is a mystery that involves a pyromaniac and there are some serial fires in the news, then use your research on the phenomenon of pyromania to write an op-ed for your local paper, or at least a letter to the editor, where you make your points, list your name and the title of your novel.

You'll be surprised how easily you can sell yourself as an expert on a topic, even if you have only written one novel about it.

Visit independent bookstores. You should go to all the independent book stores you can, bringing with you several copies of your novel. Some will take a few copies to sell, and will keep a percentage of the sale.

The management may also be interested in having you read — a way to bring customers into the store — and then you sign and sell your book in person.

Use your public libraries. Contact your local library as well as any regional libraries. Go in person to the library with your book and introduce yourself to the librarians so they can see you don't have two heads. Ask to do a reading at the library. The librarians are looking for writers to come into their library and they will be responsive to your request in most cases.

Reach out to a reporter at your local newspaper. Once you have scheduled a reading, try to gain the interest of a reporter. You can do this with emails. Send him or her a review of the book, and include something about yourself and when and where you are reading. In most cases the reporter will be interested in your personal history and why you wrote your book. You are someone noteworthy in the community.

Be determined but not obnoxious. As you begin to self-promote, don't be too aggressive. Don't be bombastic on your website or Facebook page or when you Tweet about the wonders of your novel. Yes, if you are on a radio show you should mention a good review of your book. But try to come across as a nice person, not just the writer of a just-published novel.

Get help with promotion

It takes considerable time and work to self-promote your book, but you can spend a limited amount of money and a limited amount of effort and generate significant publicity.

Purchase a listing in RTIR. Radio-TV Interview Report is a magazine that radio and television producers read to identify those who would like to be talk show guests and do free interviews to promote their books, products or causes. RTIR is sent to over 4,000 producers across the United States and Canada twice a month. Each issue lists 100–150 ads for authors and others who would like to participate in call-in or in-studio interviews. Each listing includes your ad copy (written by RTIR and subject to your approval), your book cover, and your name and phone number so that interested producers can contact you directly to arrange interviews.

To receive information about purchasing a listing in RTIR, call 1-800-553-8002 ext. 408, or go to RTIR.com to receive a media kit that includes a sample issue of the magazine and the booklet "39 Ways to Get Free Publicity As a Guest on Radio/TV Talk Shows."

But before you do any of this, remember that 40-word "selling line" you wrote on Day 89? Fiction is a tough sell, and you need to put together some ideas of what you would like to talk about during an interview that will make producers want to book you as a guest and listeners want to buy your book.

This information can also be helpful to RTIR as they draft the listing they will run about you and your book in their magazine. To promote my golf novels, I came up with the question "Is golf dying?" RTIR used this question in my ad and added the line "This Expert Reveals What Needs To Be Done to Save It . . . Now!"

And it worked! As a result of that RTIT ad, I was booked for about 20 radio interviews.

Note: To learn more about self-publishing see the "Self-publishing" listings in the next section "Resources on the Internet for Writers — A Sampling."

Resources on the Internet for Writers — *A Sampling*

Writing your novel

PW.org

This is the website of the magazine *Poets and Writers*, which describes itself as "a source of information, support, and guidance for creative writers." The website includes listings of writing contests, summer writing retreats, etc. Registration is required for access to some offerings.

AWPWriter.org

The website of the Association of Writers & Writing Programs says that it "provides support, advocacy, resources, and community" to writers. It lists centers, networks, workshops, foundations, seminars, summer conferences and other support for writers. Subscription is free, but there is a charge for some services.

Writing.com

This online community for writers of all interests and skill levels offers writing tools and opportunities for creation and inspiration, whether you are a writer looking for the perfect place to store and display your work or a reader willing to offer feedback.

DailyWritingTips.com

How to write clear, correct English.

HowStuffWorks.com

Endless info that can be helpful to writers — including such things as "slang words by decade" if your story is set in the past.

Thesaurus.com

Helps you come up with synonyms to avoid being repetitive.

After you've written your novel

AARonline.org

The Association of Authors' Representatives has a long list of agents and the genres in which they specialize.

Duotrope.com

This site claims to "make it easier for you to manage the submissions process yourself."

www.NovelPublicity.com

This is a full-service business that handles — for a fee — everything from editing and designing your novel to promoting you and your book. On the site there are also blogs with advice on writing and publishing.

EveryWritersResource.com

This website is about publishing and helping writers publish.

WritersMarket.com

This website promises to explain "where and how to sell what you write."

∎

Self publishing

groups.yahoo.com/group/Self-Publishing/

Learn a great deal about self publishing here from a community of fellow writers. Ask your questions — get answers. You must have a Yahoo account.

cnet.com/self-publishing

"Self-publishing a book: 25 things you need to know" is a very helpful article on the topic by David Carnoy

spannet.org

The Small Publishers Association of North America is very helpful for writers who are self-publishing.

ibpa-online.org

The Independent Book Publishers Association is another large professional organization for self-publishers.

IndieHousePress.org

"Professional resources for the independent voice" that include information about publishing platforms, photographers, illustrators, design & publishing services, legal & financial matters, and indie booksellers.

ParaPublishing.com

The person behind this website is Dan Poynter, author of *The Self-Publishing Manual*. The site offers many resources, both free and for sale.

en.wikipedia.org/wiki/List_of_self-publishing_companies

Self publishing companies that provide assistance in self-publishing books.

www.AutoCrit.com

First-draft editing. You can have a short sample edited as a try-out..

www.kirkusreviews.com/author-services/

Editing and review services.

www.authorbuzz.com

Marketing services.

www.PublishingGame.com

Lists of resources to help you promote your novel.

RTIR.com

Advertise your availability for interviews to promote your book on radio and TV.

www.publishersweekly.com/pw/diy/index.html

A book marketing program for self-published authors.

www.blueinkreview.com

Objective book reviews for self-published books.

▪

Self-publishing an e-book

kdp.amazon.com

Kindle Direct Publishing — To self-publish a Kindle version of your book. Includes instructions on preparing your manuscript for e-publishing, and makes your book available for purchase on Amazon.com within 24 hours after you up-load it.

▪

Terrific Books About Writing

The Art of Fiction: Notes on Craft for Young Writers by John Gardner (Vintage)

The Art of Subtext: Beyond Plot by Charles Baxter (Graywolf Press)

Bird by Bird: Some Instructions on Writing and Life by Anne Lamott (Anchor Books)

The Courage to Write: How Writers Transcend Fear by Ralph Keyes (Holt)

The Elements of Style by William Strunk and E. B. White (Longman)

How Fiction Works by James Wood (Picador)

On Becoming a Novelist by John Gardner (W. W. Norton)

Acknowledgements

For their help, edits and encouragement over
the years, I want to thank these good friends
and seasoned novelists: Mark Brazaitis, Tony
D'Souza, Robert Hamilton, Richard Lipez,
Marnie Mueller, Susan O'Neill, Mary-Ann
Tirone Smith and Jan Worth-Nelson.

I also want to thank Lisa Skelton, Gloria
Tiller of Kazoo Books, my brother Tom Coyne,
and, as always, the editor I was smart enough
to marry, Judith Coyne.

How to Write a Novel in 100 Days was designed and produced by Marian Haley Beil —
artist, book and web designer, and publisher
of PeaceCorpsWorldwide.org.

Made in the USA
San Bernardino, CA
26 April 2017